RED SYMPHONY

J. Landowsky

Translator: George Knupffer

FOREWORD

The material here given is a translation of Ch. XL of a book which appeared in Madrid in Spanish as "Sinfonía en Rojo Mayor," and is now past its 11th Edition, produced by Editorial E.R.S.A. under the well-known publisher Señor Don Mauricio Carlavilla, who has very kindly agreed to this English translation and publication. As soon as possible the full book of over 800 pp. will follow.

The given chapter is of immense importance. It is here translated from a Russian edition as well as from the Spanish. It is a complete material on its own.

The translator's own book on "The Struggle for World Power" also deals with the whole problem of super-power and global enslavement through the masters of both usury-Capitalism and terroristic Communism, which are both the tools of the same forces and serving the same purpose. The book has been published in Madrid in Spanish by Señor Carlavilla as "La Lucha por el Poder Mundial."

In the present work we see this whole story brilliantly described and proved by one of the major exponents of the subversive take-over of the world, Christian G. Rakovsky, one of the founders of Soviet Bolshevism and also a victim of the show trials just before the last war under Stalin. This is a document of historical importance and nobody who wants to be well-informed should fail to read and recommend it. Not to know the thesis here described is to know and understand nothing concerning the chief events and prospects of our time.

In the Spanish book Señor Carlavilla explains the origin of the material in question. He says:

"This is the result of a painstaking translation of several copybooks found on the body of Dr. Landowsky in a hut on the Petrograd front (Leningrad) by a Spanish volunteer.

He brought them to us. In view of the condition of the manuscripts, their restoration was a long and tiring job, lasting several years. For a long time we were not sure if they could be published. So extraordinary and unbelievable were his final disclosures that we would never have dared to publish these memoirs if the persons and events mentioned had not accorded fully with the facts.

Before these reminiscences saw the light of day we prepared ourselves for proofs and polemics. We answer fully and personally for the veracity of the basic facts.

Let us see if anyone will be able to disprove them..."

Dr. Landowsky was a Russianized Pole and lived in Russia. His father, a Colonel of the Russian Imperial Army, was shot by the Bolsheviks during the 1917 revolution. The life-story of Dr. Landowsky is astonishing. He finished the Faculty of Medicine in Russia before the revolution and then studied two years at the

Sorbonne in Paris, and he spoke fluent French. He was interested in the effects of drugs on the human organism, to help surgeons in operations. Being a talented doctor, he carried out experiments in this field and had achieved considerable results.

However, after the revolution all roads were closed to him. He lived with his family in great need, earning a living by chance jobs. Not being able to publish learned papers in his own name, he permitted a more fortunate colleague to publish them in his own name.

The all-seeing NKVD (secret police) became interested in these works and easily discovered the real author. His specialty was very valuable for them. One day in 1936 there was a knock at the doctor's door. He was invited to follow, and he was never again allowed to rejoin his family. He was placed in the building of the chemical laboratory of the NKVD near Moscow. He lived there and was forced to carry out various jobs given to him by his masters; he was a witness at questionings, tortures and the most terrible happenings and crimes. Twice he was abroad, but always under control, as a prisoner. He knew and suffered much, especially as he was a decent and religious man. He had the courage to keep notes of what he has seen and heard, and he kept whenever possible such documents and letters as passed through his hands, hiding all this in the hollow legs of his table in the chemical laboratory. So he lived until the Second World War. How he came to Petrograd and how he was killed is not known.

The document given below is an exact recorded report of the questioning of the former Ambassador in France, C.G. Rakovsky during the period of the trials of the Trotskyists in the USSR in 1938, when he was tried together with Bukharin, Rykoff, Yagoda, Karakhan, Dr. Levin and others.

Insofar as the accused Rakovsky made it clear, having in mind the sparing of his life, that he could give information about matters of very special interest, Stalin gave orders to his foreign agent to carry out the questioning.

It is known that Rakovsky was sentenced to be shot, like the others, but was reprieved and given 20 years of prison.

Very interesting is the description of the above mentioned agent. This was a certain René Duval (also known as Gavriil Gavriilovitch Kus'min), the son of a millionaire, very good looking and talented. He studied in France. His widowed mother adored him. But the young man was carried away by Communist propaganda and fell into the hands of their agency. They suggested that he should study in Moscow, and he gladly accepted the proposal. He passed through the severe school of the NKVD and became a foreign agent, and when he wanted to change his mind, it was too late. They do not let people out of their grip. By the exercise of will-power he reached the "heights of evil," as he called it, and enjoyed the full confidence of Stalin himself.

The questioning took place in French by this agent. The doctor was present in order to put drug pills unnoticed into the glass of Rakovsky, to induce energy and a good mood. Behind the wall the conversation was registered on apparatus, and the technician who operated it did not understand French. Then Dr. Landowsky had to translate into Russian, with two copies, for Stalin and Gabriel. Secretly he dared to make a carbon copy, which he hid anyway.

* * *
XL
X-RAY OF REVOLUTION

I returned to the laboratory. My nervous system bothered me and I prescribed myself complete rest. I am in bed almost the whole day. Here I am quite alone for already four days. Gabriel enquired about me every day. He has to reckon with my condition. At the mere thought that they could again send me to the Lubianka (Moscow HQ of the secret police) to be present at a new scene of terror I become excited and tremble. I am ashamed of belonging to the human race. How low have people fallen! How low have I fallen!

* * *

These lines are all I was able to write after five days following my return from the Lubianka, when trying to describe on paper the horror, and thereby interrupting the chronological order of my notes. I could not write. Only after several months, when summer began, I was able calmly and simply to set out all that I had seen, disgusting, vicious, evil...

During these past months I asked myself a thousand times the same question: "Who were the people who were anonymously present at the torture?" I strained all my intuitive and deductive capabilities. Was it Ezhov? It is possible, but I see no reason why he should have concealed himself. Officially he is responsible and the fear which made him hide does not lead to a logical explanation. Even more: if I have any reason for describing myself as a psychologist, then this fanatic, the chief of the NKVD, with signs of abnormality, would be certain to enjoy a criminal display. Such things as the expression of haughtiness in front of a humbled enemy, who had been converted into a wreck psychologically and physically, should have given him an unhealthy pleasure. I analyzed still further. The absence of prior preparation was obvious; evidently the decision to call this satanic session had been taken in a hurry. The circumstance that I had been appointed to be present was the result of a sudden agreement. If Ezhov had been able to choose the time freely, then timely preparations would have been made. And then I would not have been called; that general of the NKVD who was hardly able to come in time, for the purpose of being present at the torture, would have known about this beforehand. If this was not Ezhov, then who had decided on the time? Which other chief was able to arrange it all? However poor are my informations about the Soviet hierarchy, but above Ezhov in affairs along the line of the NKVD there is only one man— Stalin. Therefore it was he?...

Asking myself these questions, which arose from my deductions, I remembered yet other facts in support of my opinion. I remembered that when I looked from the window over the square a few minutes before we went down to the "spectacle" I saw how there drove across it four large identical cars; all we Soviet people know that Stalin travels in a caravan of identical machines, so that nobody would know in which he is sitting, to make attack more difficult. Was he there?...

But here I came across another mystery: according to the details which Gabriel gave me, the hidden observers were to sit behind our back. But there I could only see a long mirror, through which nothing could be seen. Perhaps it was transparent? I was puzzled.

* * *

Only seven days passed when one morning Gabriel appeared in the house. I found that he had an energetic and enthusiastic appearance and was in an optimistic mood. Yet these flashes of happiness which lit up his face at first, did not return later. It seemed as if he wanted chase away the shadows which passed over his face by increased activity and mental exertion.

After lunch he told me:

"We have a guest here."

"Who is it" I asked.

"Rakovsky, the former Ambassador in Paris."

"I do not know him."

"He is one of those whom I pointed out to you on that night; the former Ambassador in London and Paris... Of course a big friend of your acquaintance Navachin... Yes, this man is at my disposal. He is here with us; he is being well treated and looked after. You shall see him."

"I, why? You know well that I am not curious about matters of this kind... I would ask you to spare me this sight; I am still not quite well after what you had forced me to see. I cannot guarantee my nervous system and heart."

"Oh, do not worry. Now we are not concerned with force. This man has already been broken. No blood, no force. It is only necessary to give him moderate doses of drugs. Here I have brought you details: they are from Levin* who still serves us with his knowledge. Apparently there is a certain drug somewhere in the laboratory, which can work wonders."

"You believe all this?"

"I am speaking in symbolic form. Rakovsky is inclined to confess to everything he knows about the matter. We have already had a preliminary talk with him, and the results are not bad."

"In that case why is there a need for a miraculous drug?"

"You will see, doctor, you will see. This is a small safety measure, dictated by the professional experience of Levin. It will help to achieve that our man being questioned would feel optimistic and would not lose hope and faith. He can already see a chance of saving his life as a long shot. This is the first effect which we must attain. Then we must make sure that he would all the time remain in a state of the experience of the decisive happy moment, but without losing his mental capacities; more exactly, it will be necessary to stimulate and sharpen them. He must have induced in him a quite special feeling. How can one express it? More exactly a condition of enlightened stimulation."

"Something like hypnosis?"

"Yes, but without sleepiness."

"And I must invent a drug for all this? I think you exaggerate my scientific talents. I cannot achieve it."

* Former NKVD doctor, was a co-defendant with Rakovsky at the trial.

"Yes, but it is unnecessary to invent anything, doctor. As for Levin, he asserts that the problem has already been solved."

"He always left me with the impression of being something of a charlatan…"

"Probably yes, but I think that the drug he has mentioned, even if it is not as effective as he claims, will still help us to achieve the necessary; after all, we need not expect a miracle. Alcohol, against our will, makes us speak nonsense. Why cannot another substance encourage us to say the reasonable truth? Apart from that, Levin had told me of previous cases, which seem to be genuine."

"Why do you not want to force him to take part in this affair once more? Or will he refuse to obey?"

"Oh no, he would like to. It is enough to want to save or to extend your life with the help of this or another service, for not refusing. But it is I myself who does not want to use his services. He must not hear anything of that which Rakovsky will tell me. Not he, not anyone…"

"Therefore I…"

"You— that is another matter, doctor. You are a deeply decent person. But I am not Diogenes, to rush to look for another over the snowy distances of the USSR."

"Thank you, but I think that my honesty…"

"Yes, doctor, yes; you say that we take advantage of your honesty for various depravities. Yes, doctor, that is so…; but it is only so from your absurd point of view. And who is attracted today by absurdities? For example such an absurdity as your honesty? You always manage to lead one away towards conversation about most attractive things. But what, in fact, will take place? You must only help me to give the correct doses of Levin's drug. It would appear that in the dosage there is an invisible line which divides sleep from a state of activity, a clear condition from a befogged one, good sense from nonsense…; there can come an artificial excessive enthusiasm."

"If that is all…"

"And yet something else. Now we shall speak seriously. Study the instructions of Levin, weigh them, adapt them reasonably to the condition and strength of the prisoner. You have time for study until nightfall; you can examine Rakovsky as often as you wish. And that is all for the moment. You would not believe how terribly I want to sleep. I shall sleep a few hours. If by evening nothing extraordinary happens then I have given instructions that I am not to be called. I would advise you to have a good rest after dinner, because after that it will not be possible to sleep for a long time."

We entered the vestibule. Having taken his leave from me he quickly ran up the stairs, but in the middle he halted.

"Ah, doctor – he exclaimed – I had forgotten. Many thanks from Comrade Ezhov. Expect a present, perhaps even a decoration."

He waved me goodbye and rapidly disappeared on the staircase landing of the top floor.

* * *

The notes of Levin were short, but clear and exact. I had no difficulty in finding the medicine. It was in doses of a milligram in tiny tablets. I made a test and, in accordance with his explanation, they dissolved very easily in water and better still in alcohol. The formula was not indicated there, and I decided later to make a detailed analysis, when I shall have the time.

Undoubtedly it was some substance of the specialist Lumenstadt, that scientist of whom Levin had spoken to me during the first meeting. I did not think I would discover during analysis something unexpected or new. Probably again some base with a considerable amount of opium of a more active kind than tebain. I was well acquainted with 19 main types and some more besides. In those practical conditions in which my experiments were conducted I was satisfied with those facts which my investigations had yielded.

Although my work had an altogether different direction, yet I was quite at home in the realm of hallucinatory substances. I remembered that Levin had told me of the distillation of rare types of Indian Hemp. I was bound to be dealing with opium or hashish, in order to penetrate the secret of this much praised drug. I would have been glad to have had the opportunity of coming across one or more new bases which gave rise to his "miraculous" qualities. In principle I was prepared to assume such a possibility. After all the work of investigation in conditions of unlimited time and means, while not having to reckon with economic limitations, which was possible in conditions of the NKVD, provided unlimited scientific possibilities. I flattered myself with the illusion of being able to find, as the result of these investigations, a new weapon in my scientific fight against pain.

I could not give much time to the diversion of such pleasant illusions. I concentrated my thoughts in order to think how and in what proportion I shall have to give Rakovsky this drug. According to the instructions of Levin, one tablet would have to produce the desired result. He warned that if the patient had any heart weakness there could follow sleepiness and even complete lethargy, with a consequent dimming of the mind. While bearing all this in mind, I had first of all to examine Rakovsky. I did not expect to find the internal condition of his heart to be normal. If there were no damage, then surely there would be a lowering of tone as the result of the nervous experiences, as his system could not have remained unchanged after a long and terrifying torture.

I put off the examination until after lunch. I wanted to consider everything, both for the case that Gabriel would want to give the drug with the knowledge of Rakovsky, as also without his knowledge. In both cases I would have to busy myself with him, insofar as I myself would have to give him the drug of which I had been told concretely. There was no need for the participation of a professional, as the drug was given by mouth.

After lunch I went to visit Rakovsky. He was kept locked up in one room of the ground floor and was guarded by one man, who did not take his eyes off him. Of furniture there was only one small table, a narrow bed without ends and another small, rough table. When I entered Rakovsky was sitting. He immediately got up. He looked at me closely and I read in his face doubt and, it seemed, also fright. I think he must have recognized me, having seen me when he sat that memorable night at the side of the generals.

I ordered the guard to leave and told him to bring me a chair. I sat down and asked the prisoner to sit. He was about 50 years old. He was a man of medium height, bald in front, with a large, fleshy nose. In youth his face was probably pleasant. His facial outlines were not typically semitic, but his origin was nevertheless clear. Once upon a time he was probably quite fat, but not now, and his skin hung everywhere, while his face and neck were like a burst balloon, with the air let out. The usual dinner at the Lubianka was apparently too strict a diet for the former Ambassador in Paris. At that moment I made no further observations.

"You smoke?" I asked, opening the cigarette case, with the intention of establishing somewhat more intimate relations with him.

"I gave up smoking in order to preserve my health" he replied with a very pleasant tone of voice, "but I thank you; I think I have now recovered from my stomach troubles."

He smoked quietly, with restraint and not without some elegance.

"I am a doctor" I introduced myself.

"Yes I know that; I saw how you acted 'there' " he said with trembling voice.

"I came to enquire about the state of your health. How are you? Do you suffer from any illness?"

"No, nothing."

"Are you sure? What about your heart?"

"Thanks to the results of enforced dieting I do not observe in myself any abnormal symptoms."

"There are some which cannot be noticed by the patient himself, but only by a doctor."

"I am a doctor" he interrupted me. "A doctor?" I repeated in surprise. "Yes, didn't you know?"

"Nobody had told me of it. I congratulate you. I shall be very glad to be of use to a colleague and, possibly, a fellow student. Where did you study? In Moscow or Petrograd?"

"Oh no! At that time I was not a Russian subject. I studied in Nancy and Montpellier; in the latter I received my doctorate."

"This means that we may have studied at the same time; I did several courses in Paris. Were you French?"

"I intended to become French. I was born a Bulgarian, but without asking my permission I was converted into a Rumanian. My province was Dobrudga, where I was born, and after the peace treaty it went to Rumania."

"Permit me to listen to your chest"— and I put the stethoscope in my ears.

He took off his torn jacket and stood up. I listened. The examination showed nothing abnormal; as I had assumed, weakness, but without defects.

"I suppose one must give food for the heart."

"Only the heart, comrade?" he asked ironically.

"I think so" I said, pretending not to have noticed the irony, "I think your diet, too, should be strengthened."

"Permit me to listen to myself."

"With pleasure"— and I gave him the stethoscope.

He quickly listened to himself.

"I had expected that my condition would be much worse. Many thanks. May I put my jacket on?"

"Of course. Let us agree, then, that it is necessary to take a few drops of digitalis, don't you think?"

"You consider that absolutely essential? I think that my old heart will survive the few days or months which remain to me quite well."

"I think otherwise; I think that you will live much longer."

"Do not upset me, colleague… To live more! To live still longer!… There must be instructions about the end; the court case cannot last longer... And then, then rest."

And when he said this, having in mind the final rest, it seemed that his face had the expression of happiness almost. I shuddered. This wish to die, to die soon which I read in his eyes, made me faint. I wanted to cheer him up from a feeling of compassion.

"You have not understood me, comrade. I wanted to say that in your case it may be decided to continue your life, but life without suffering. For what have you been brought here? Does one not treat you well now?"

"The latter, yes, of course. Concerning the rest I have heard hints, but…" I gave him another cigarette and then added:

"Have hope. For my part and to the extent which my chief will allow, I shall do everything that can depend on me, to make sure that you come to no harm. I shall begin immediately by feeding you, but not excessively, bearing in mind the state of your stomach. We shall begin with a milk diet and some more substantial additions. I shall give instructions at once. You may smoke… take some… " and I left him everything that remained in the packet.

I called the guard and ordered him to light the prisoner's cigarette whenever he wants to smoke. Then I left and before having a couple of hours rest I gave instructions that Rakovsky was to have half a liter of milk with sugar.

* * *

We prepared for the meeting with Rakovsky at midnight. Its "friendly" character was stressed in all the details. The room was well warmed, there was a fire in the fire-place, soft lighting, a small and well-chosen supper, good wines; all had been scientifically improvised. "As for a lovers meeting," observed Gabriel. I was to assist. My chief responsibility was to give the prisoner the drug in such a manner that he would not notice it. For this purpose the drinks had been placed as if by chance near me, and I shall have to pour out the wine. Also I would have to observe the weakening of the drug's effect, so as to give a new dose at the right moment. This was my most important job. Gabriel wants, if the experiment succeeds, to get already at the first meeting real progress towards the essence of the matter. He is hopeful of success. He has had a good rest and is in good condition. I am interested to know how he will struggle with Rakovsky who, it seems to me, is an opponent worthy of him.

Three large arm-chairs were placed before the fire. The one nearest the door is for me, Rakovsky will sit in the middle, and in the third will be Gabriel, who had shown his optimistic mood even in his clothes, as he was wearing a white Russian shirt.

It had already struck midnight when they brought the prisoner to us. He had been given decent clothes and had been well shaved. I looked at him professionally and found him to be livelier.

He asks to be excused for not being able to drink more than one glass, mentioning the weakness of his stomach. I did not put the drug into this glass and regretted it.

The conversation began with banalities... Gabriel knows that Rakovsky speaks much better French than Russian and begins in that language. There are hints about the past. It is clear that Rakovsky is an expert conversationalist. His speech is exact, elegant and even decorative. He is apparently very erudite; at times he quotes easily and always accurately. Sometimes he hints at his many escapes, at exile, about Lenin, Plekhanov, Luxemburg, and he even said that when he was a boy he had shaken the hand of the old Engels.

We drink whisky. After Gabriel had given him the opportunity of speaking for about half an hour, I asked as if by chance: "Should I add more soda water?" "Yes, add enough" he replied absentmindedly. I manipulated the drink and dropped a tablet into it, which I had been holding from the very beginning. First I gave Gabriel some whisky, letting him know by a sign that the job had been done. I gave Rakovsky his glass and then began to drink mine. He sipped it with pleasure. "I am a small cad" I told myself. But this was a passing thought and it dissolved in the pleasant fire in the fireplace.

Before Gabriel came to the main theme, the talk had been long and interesting.

I had been fortunate in obtaining a document which reproduces better than a shorthand note all that had been discussed between Gabriel and Rakovsky. Here it is:

INFORMATION
THE QUESTIONING OF THE ACCUSED CHRISTIAN GEORGIEVITCH RAKOVSKY BY GAVRIIL GAVRIILOVITCH KUS'MIN ON THE 26TH JANUARY, 1938.

Gavriil G. Kus'min— In accordance with our agreement at the Lubianka, I had appealed for a last chance for you; your presence in this house indicates that I had succeeded in this. Let us see if you will not deceive us.

Christian G. Rakovsky— I do not wish and shall not do that.

G – But first of all: a well-meant warning. Now we are concerned with the real truth. Not the "official" truth, that which is to figure at the trial in the light of the confessions of the accused... This is something which, as you know, is fully subject to practical considerations or "considerations of State" as they would say in the West. The demands of international politics will force us to hide the whole truth, the "real truth"... Whatever may be the course of the trial, but governments and peoples will only be told that which they should know. But he who must know everything, Stalin, must also know all this. Therefore, whatever may be your words here they cannot make your position worse. You must know that they will not worsen your crime but, on the contrary, they can give the desired results in your favor. You will be able to save your life, which at this moment is already lost. So now I have told you this, but now let us see: you will all admit that you are Hitler's spies and receive wages from the Gestapo and OKW.*

Is that not so?

R – Yes.

G – And you are Hitler's spies?

R – Yes.

G – No, Rakovsky, no. Tell the real truth, but not the court proceedings one.

R – We are not spies of Hitler, we hate Hitler as you can hate him, as Stalin can hate him; perhaps even more so, but this is a very complex question.

G – I shall help you... By chance I also know one or two things. You, the Trotskyists, had contacts with the German Staff. Is that not so?

R – Yes.

G – From which period?

R – I do not know the exact date, but soon after the fall of Trotsky. Of course before Hitler's coming to power.

G – Therefore let us be exact: you were neither personal spies of Hitler, nor of his regime.

R – Exactly. We were such already earlier.

G – And for what purpose? With the aim of giving Germany victory and some Russian territories?

R – No, in no case.

G – Therefore as ordinary spies, for money?

R – For money? Nobody received a single Mark from Germany. Hitler has not enough money to buy, for example, the Commissar for Foreign Affairs of the USSR, who has at his disposal freely a budget which is greater than the total wealth of Morgan and Vanderbilt, and who does not have to account for his use of the money.

G – Well, then for what reason?

R – May I speak quite freely?

G – Yes, I ask you to do so; for that reason you have been invited.

R – Did not Lenin have higher aims when he received help from Germany in order to enter Russia? And is it necessary to accept as true those libelous inventions which had been circulated to accuse him? Was he not also called a spy of the Kaiser? His relations with the Emperor and the German intervention in the affair of the sending to Russia of the Bolshevik destroyers are quite clear

---

*OKW— Oberkommando der Wehrmacht, Supreme Command of the German Army — Transl.

G – Whether it is true or not does not have any bearing on the present question.

R – No, permit me to finish. Is it not a fact that the activity of Lenin was in the beginning advantageous to the German troops? Permit me… There was the separate peace of Brest-Litovsk, at which huge territories of the USSR were ceded to Germany. Who had declared defeatism as a weapon of the Bolsheviks in 1913? Lenin. I know by heart his words from his letter to Gorky: "War between Austria and Russia would be a most useful thing for the revolution, but it is hardly possible that Francis-Joseph and Nicholas would present us with this opportunity." As you see, we, the so-called Trotskyists, the inventors of the defeat in 1905, continue at the present stage the same line, the line of Lenin.

G – With a small difference, Rakovsky; at present there is Socialism in the USSR, not the Tsar.

R – You believe that?

G – What?

R – In the existence of Socialism in the USSR?

G – Is the Soviet Union not Socialist?

R – For me only in name. It is just here that we find the true reason for the opposition. Agree with me, and by the force of pure logic you must agree, that theoretically, rationally, we have the same right to say – no, as Stalin can say – yes. And if for the triumph of Communism defeatism can be justified, then he who considers that Communism has been destroyed by the Bonapartism of Stalin and that he betrayed it, has the same right as Lenin to become a defeatist.

G – I think, Rakovsky, that you are theorizing thanks to your manner of making wide use of dialectics. It is clear that if many people were present here, I would prove this; all right, I accept your argument as the only one possible in your position, but nevertheless I think that I could prove to you that this is nothing other than a sophism. But let us postpone this for another occasion; someday it will come. And I hope that you will give me the chance to reply. But at the present moment I shall only say this: if your defeatism and the defeat of the USSR has as its object the restoration of Socialism in the USSR, real Socialism, according to you— Trotskyism, then, insofar as we have destroyed their leaders and cadres, defeatism and the defeat of the USSR has neither an objective nor any sense. As a result of defeat now there would come the enthronement of some Führer or fascist Tsar. Is that not so?

R – It is true. Without flattery on my part— your deduction is splendid.

G – Well, if, as I assume, you assert this sincerely, then we have achieved a great deal: I am a Stalinist and you a Trotskyist; we have achieved the impossible. We have reached the point at which our views coincide. The coincidence lies in that at the present moment the USSR must not be destroyed.

R – I must confess that I had not expected to face such a clever person. In fact at the present stage and for some years we cannot think of the defeat of the USSR and to provoke it, as it is known that we are at present in such a position, that we cannot seize power. We, the Communists, would derive no profit from it. This is exact and coincides with your view. We cannot be interested now in the collapse of the

Stalinist State; I say this and at the same time I assert that this State, apart from all that has been said, is anti- Communistic. You see that I am sincere.

G – I see that. This is the only way in which we can come to terms. I would ask you, before you continue, to explain to me that which seems to me a contradiction: if the Soviet State is anti-Communistic to you, then why should you not wish its destruction at the given moment? Someone else might be less anti-Communistic and then there would be fewer obstacles to the restoration of your pure Communism.

R – No, no, this deduction is too simple. Although the Stalinist Bonapartism also opposes Communism as the Napoleonic one opposed the revolution, but the circumstance is clear that, nevertheless, the USSR continues to preserve its Communistic form and dogma; this is formal and not real Communism. And thus, like the disappearance of Trotsky gave Stalin the possibility automatically to transform real Communism into the formal one, so also the disappearance of Stalin will allow us to transform his formal Communism into a real one. One hour would suffice for us. Have you understood me?

G – Yes, of course; you have told us the classical truth that nobody destroys that which he wants to inherit. Well, all right; all else is sophistical agility. You rely on the assumption which can be easily disproved: the assumption of Stalin's anti-Communism. Is there private property in the USSR? Is there personal profit? Classes? I shall not continue to base myself on facts— for what?

R – I have already agreed that there exists formal Communism. All that you enumerate are merely forms.

G – Yes? For what purpose? From mere obstinacy?

R – Of course not. This is a necessity. It is impossible to eliminate the materialistic evolution of history. The most that can be done is to hold it up. And at what a price? At the cost of its theoretical acceptance, in order to destroy it in practice. The force which draws humanity towards Communism is so unconquerable that that same force, but distorted, opposed to itself, can only achieve a slowing down of development; more accurately— to slow down the progress of the permanent revolution.

G – An example?

R – The most obvious— with Hitler. He needed Socialism for victory over Socialism: it is this his very anti-Socialist Socialism which is National-Socialism. Stalin needs Communism in order to defeat Communism. The parallel is obvious. But, notwithstanding Hitler's anti-Socialism and Stalin's anti-Communism, both, to their regret and against their will, transcendentally create Socialism and Communism…; they and many others. Whether they want it or not, whether they know it or not, but they create formal Socialism and Communism, which we, the Communist-Marxists, must inevitably inherit.

G – Inheritance? Who inherits? Trotskyism is completely liquidated.

R – Although you say so, you do not believe it. However great may be the liquidations, we Communists will survive them. The long arm of Stalin and his police cannot reach all Communists.

G – Rakovsky, I ask you, and if necessary command, to refrain from offensive hints. Do not go too far in taking advantage of your "diplomatic immunity."

R – Do I have credentials? Whose ambassador am I?

G – Precisely of that unreachable Trotskyism, if we agree to call him so.

R – I cannot be a diplomat of Trotskyism, of which you hint. I have not been given that right to represent it, and I have not taken this role on myself. You have given it to me.

G – I begin to trust you. I take note in your favor that at my hint about this Trotskyism you did not deny it. This is already a good beginning.

R – But how can I deny it? After all, I myself mentioned it.

G – Insofar as we have recognized the existence of this special Trotskyism by our mutual arrangement, I want you to give definite facts, which are necessary for the investigation of the given coincidence.

R – Yes, I shall be able to mention that which you consider necessary to know and I shall do it on my own initiative, but I shall not be able to assert that this is always the thinking also of "Them."

G – Yes, I shall look on it like that.

R – We agreed that at the present moment the opposition cannot be interested in defeatism and the fall of Stalin, insofar as we do not have the physical possibility of taking his place. This is what we both agree. At present this is an incontrovertible fact. However, there is in existence a possible aggressor. There he is, that great nihilist Hitler, who is aiming with his terrible weapon of the Wehrmacht at the whole horizon. Whether we want it or not, but he will use it against the USSR? Let us agree that for us this is the decisive unknown factor, do you consider that the problem has been correctly stated?

G – It has been well put. But I can say that for me there is no unknown factor consider the attack of Hitler on the USSR to be inevitable.

R – Why?

G – Very simple; because he who controls it is inclined towards attack. Hitler is only the condottiere of international Capitalism.

R – I agree that there is a danger, but from that to the assumption on this ground of the inevitability of his attack on the USSR— there is a whole abyss.

G – The attack on the USSR is determined by the very essence of Fascism. In addition he is impelled towards it by all those Capitalist States which had allowed him to re-arm and to take all the necessary economic and strategic bases. This is quite obvious.

R – You forget something very important. The re-armament of Hitler and the assistance he received at the present time from the Versailles nations (take good note of this)— were received by him during a special period, when we could still have become the heirs of Stalin in the case of his defeat, when the opposition still existed... Do you consider this fact to be a matter of chance or only a coincidence in time?

G – I do not see any connection between the permission of the Versailles Powers of German re-armament and the existence of the opposition... The trajectory of

Hitlerism is in itself clear and logical. The attack on the USSR was part of his program already a long time ago. The destruction of Communism and expansion in the East— these are dogmas from the book "Mein Kampf," that Talmud of National-Socialism..., but that your defeatists wanted to take advantage of this threat to the USSR that is, of course, in accordance with your train of thought.

R – Yes, at a first glance this appears to be natural and logical, too logical and natural for the truth.

G – To prevent this happening, so that Hitler would not attack us, we would have to entrust ourselves to an alliance with France..., but that would be a naïveté. It would mean that we believe that Capitalism would be willing to make sacrifices for the sake of saving Communism.

R – If we shall continue the discussion only on the foundation of those conceptions which apply for use at mass meetings, then you are quite right. But if you are sincere in saying this then, forgive me, I am disappointed; I had thought that the politics of the famous Stalinist police stand on a higher level.

G – The Hitlerist attack on the USSR is, in addition, a dialectical necessity; it is the same as the inevitable struggle of the classes in the international plane. At the side of Hitler, inevitably, there will stand the whole global Capitalism.

R – And so, believe me, that in the light of your scholastic dialectics, I have formed a very negative opinion about the political culture of Stalinism. I listen to your words as Einstein could listen to a schoolboy talking about physics in four dimensions. I see that you are only acquainted with elementary Marxism, i.e. with the demagogic, popular one.

G – If your explanation will not be too long and involved, I should be grateful to you for some explanation of this "relativity" or "quantum" of Marxism.

R – Here there is no irony; I am speaking with the best intentions... In this same elementary Marxism, which is taught even in your Stalinist University, you can find the statement which contradicts the whole of your thesis about the inevitability of the Hitlerist attack on the USSR. You are also taught that the cornerstone of Marxism is the assertion that, supposedly, contradictions are the incurable and fatal illness of Capitalism... Is that not so?

G – Yes, of course.

R – But if things are in fact such that we accuse Capitalism of being imbued with continuous Capitalistic contradictions in the sphere of economics, then why should it necessarily suffer from them also in politics? The political and economic is of no importance in itself; this is a condition or measurement of the social essence, but contradictions arise in the social sphere, and are reflected simultaneously in the economic or political ones, or in both at the same time. It would be absurd to assume fallibility in economics and simultaneously infallibility in politics— which is something essential in order that an attack on the USSR should become inevitable – according to your postulate – absolutely essential.

G – This means that you rely in everything on the contradictions, fatality and inevitability of the errors which must be committed by the bourgeoisie, which will hinder Hitler from attacking the USSR. I am a Marxist, Rakovsky, but here, between ourselves, in order not to provide the pretext for anger to a single activist, I say to you that with all my faith in Marx I would not believe that the USSR exists thanks to the mistakes of its enemies... And I think that Stalin shares the same view.

R – But I do think so... Do not look at me like that, as I am not joking and am not mad.

G – Permit me at least to doubt it, until you will have proved your assertions.

R – Do you now see that I had reasons for qualifying your Marxist culture as being doubtful? Your arguments and reactions are the same as any rank and file activist.

G – And they are wrong?

R – Yes, they are correct for a small administrator, for a bureaucrat and for the mass. They suit the average fighter... They must believe this and repeat everything as it has been written. Listen to me by way of the completely confidential. With Marxism you get the same results as with the ancient esoteric religions. Their adherents had to know only that which was the most elementary and crude, insofar as by this one provoked their faith, i.e. that which is absolutely essential, both in religion and in the work of revolution.

G – Do you not now want to open up to me the mystical Marxism, something like yet another freemasonry?

R – No, no esoterics. On the contrary, I shall explain it with the maximal clarity. Marxism, before being a philosophical, economic and political system, is a conspiracy for the revolution. And as for us the revolution is the only absolute reality, it follows that philosophy, economics and politics are true only insofar as they lead to revolution. The fundamental truth (let us call it subjective) does not exist in economics, politics or even morals: in the light of scientific abstraction it is either truth or error, but for us, who are subject to revolutionary dialectic, it is only truth. And insofar as to us, who are subject to revolutionary dialectic, it is only truth, and therefore the sole truth, then it must be such for all that is revolutionary, and such it was to Marx. In accordance with this we must act. Remember the phrase of Lenin, in reply to someone who demonstrated by way of argument that, supposedly, his intention contradicted reality: "I feel it to be real" was his answer. Do you not think that Lenin spoke nonsense? No, for him every reality; every truth was relative in the face of the sole and absolute one: the revolution. Marx was a genius. If his works had amounted to only the deep criticism of Capitalism, then even that would have been an unsurpassed scientific work; but in those places where his writing reaches the level of mastery, there comes the effect of an apparently ironical work. "Communism" he says "must win because Capital will give it that victory, though its enemy." Such is the magisterial thesis of Marx......Can there be a greater irony? And then, in order that he should be believed, it was enough for him to depersonalize Capitalism and Communism, having transformed the human individual into a consciously thinking individual, which he did with the extraordinary talent of a juggler. Such was his sly method, in order to demonstrate to the Capitalists that they are a reality of Capitalism and that Communism can triumph as the result of inborn idiocy; since without the presence of immortal idiocy in *homo economico* there could not appear in him continuous contradictions as proclaimed by Marx. To be able to achieve the transformation of *homo sapiens* into *homo stultum* is to possess magical force, capable of bringing man down to the first stage of the zoological ladder, i.e. to the level of the animal. Only if there is *homo stultum* in the epoch of the apogee of Capitalism could Marx formulate his axiomatic proposition: contradictions plus time equal Communism. Believe me, when we who are initiated into this, contemplate the representation of Marx, for example the one which is placed above the main entrance to the Lubianka, then we cannot prevent the inner explosion of laughter by which Marx had infected us; we see how he laughs into his beard at all humanity.

G – And you are still capable of laughing at the most revered scientist of the epoch?

R – Ridicule, me?... This is the highest admiration! In order that Marx should be able to deceive so many people of science, it was essential that he should tower above them all. Well: in order to have judgments about Marx in all his greatness, we must consider the real Marx, Marx the revolutionary, Marx, judged by his manifesto. This means Marx the conspirator, as during his life the revolution was in a condition of conspiracy. It is not for nothing that the revolution is indebted for its development and its recent victories to these conspirators.

G – Therefore you deny the existence of the dialectical process of contradictions in Capitalism, which lead to the final triumph of Communism ?

R – You can be sure that if Marx believed that Communism will achieve victory only thanks to the contradictions in Capitalism, then he would not have once, never, mentioned the contradictions on the thousands of pages of his scientific revolutionary work. Such was the categorical imperative of the realistic nature of Marx: not the scientific, but the revolutionary one. The revolutionary and conspirator will never disclose to his opponent the secret of his triumph... He would never give the information; he would give him disinformation which you use in counter-conspiracy. Is that not so?

G – However, in the end we have reached the conclusion (according to you) that there are no contradictions in Capitalism, and if Marx speaks of them then it is only a revolutionary-strategic method. That is so? But the colossal and ever-growing contradictions in Capitalism are there to see. And so we get the conclusion that Marx, having lied, spoke the truth.

R – You are dangerous as a dialectician, when you destroy the brakes of scholastic dogmatism and give free rein to your own inventiveness. So it is, that Marx spoke the truth when he lied. He lied when he led into error, having defined the contradictions as being "continuous" in the history of the economics of capital and called them "natural and inevitable," but at the same time he stated the truth because he knew that the contradictions would be created and would grow in an increasing progression until they reach their apogee.

G – This means that with you there is an antithesis?

R – There is no antithesis here. Marx deceives for tactical reasons about the origin of the contradictions in Capitalism, but not about their obvious reality. Marx knew how they were created, how they became more acute and how things went towards general anarchy in Capitalistic production, which came before the triumph of the Communist revolution... He knew it would happen because he knew those who created the contradictions.

G – It is a very strange revelation and piece of news, this assertion and exposal of the circumstance that that which leads Capitalism to its "suicide," by the well-chosen expression of the bourgeois economist Schmalenbach, in support of Marx, is not the essence and inborn law of Capitalism. But I am interested to know if we will reach the personal by this path?

R – Have you not felt this intuitively? Have you not noticed how in Marx words contradict deeds? He declares the necessity and inevitability of Capitalist contradictions, proving the existence of surplus value and accumulation, i.e. he proves that which really exists. He nimbly invents the proposition that to a greater concentration of the means of production corresponds a greater mass of the proletariat, a greater force for the building of Communism, is that not so? Now go on: at the same time as this assertion he founds the International. Yet the International is, in the work of the daily struggle of the classes, a "reformist," i.e. an organization whose purpose is the limitation of the surplus value and, where possible, its elimination. For this reason, objectively, the International is a counter-revolutionary organization and anti-Communist, in accordance with Marx's theory.

G – Now we get that Marx is a counter-revolutionary and an anti-Communist.

R – Well, now you see how one can make use of the original Marxist culture. It is only possible to describe the International as being counter-revolutionary and anti-Communist, with logical and scientific exactness, if one does not see in the facts anything more than the directly visible result and in the texts only the letter. One comes to such absurd conclusions, while they seem to be obvious, when one forgets that words and facts in Marxism are subject to strict rules of the higher science: the rules of conspiracy and revolution.

G – Will we ever reach the final conclusions?

R – In a moment. If the class struggle, in the economic sphere, turns out to be reformist in the light of its first results, and for that reason contradicts the theoretical presuppositions, which determine the establishment of Communism, then it is, in its real and true meaning, purely revolutionary. But I repeat again: it is subject to the rules of conspiracy, that means to masking and the hiding of its true aims... The limitation of the surplus value and thus also of accumulations as the consequence of the class struggle— that is only a matter of appearances, an illusion, in order to stimulate the basic revolutionary movement in the masses. A strike is already an attempt at revolutionary mobilization. Independently of whether it wins or not, its economic effect is anarchical. As a result this method for the improvement of the economic position of one class brings about the impoverishment of the economy in general; whatever may be the scale and results of the strike, it will always bring about a reduction of production. The general result: more poverty, which the working class cannot shake off. That is already something. But that is not the only result and not the most important one. As we know, the only aim of any struggle in the economic sphere is to earn more and work less. Such is the economic absurdity, but according to our terminology, such is the contradiction, which has not been noticed by the masses, which are blinded at any given moment by a rise in wages, which is at once annulled by a rise in prices. And if prices are limited by governmental action, then the same thing happens, i.e. a contradiction between the wish to spend more, produce less, is qualified here by monetary inflation. And so one gets a vicious circle: a strike, hunger, inflation, hunger.

G – With the exception when the strike takes place at the expense of the surplus value of Capitalism.

R – Theory, pure theory. Speaking between ourselves, take any annual handbook concerning the economics of any country and divide rents and the total income by all those receiving wages or salaries, and you will see what an extraordinary result emerges. This result is the most counter-revolutionary fact, and we must keep it a complete secret. This is because if you deduct from the theoretical dividend the salaries and expenses of the directors, which would be the consequence on the abolition of ownership, then almost always there remains a dividend which is a debit for the proletariat. In reality always a debit, if we also consider the reduction in the volume and quality of production. As you will now see, a call to strike, as a means for achieving a quick improvement of the well-being of the proletariat is only an excuse; an excuse required in order to force it to commit sabotage of Capitalistic production. Thus to the contradictions in the bourgeois system are added contradictions within the proletariat; this is the double weapon of the revolution, and it – which is obvious – does not arise of itself: there exists an organization, chiefs, discipline, and above that there exists stupidity. Don't you suspect that the much-mentioned contradictions of Capitalism, and in particular the financial ones, are also organized by someone?... By way of basis for these deductions I shall remind you that in its economic struggle the proletarian International coincides with the financial International, since both produce inflation, and wherever there is coincidence there, one should assume, is also agreement. Those are his own words.

G – I suspect here such an enormous absurdity, or the intention of spinning a new paradox, that I do not want to imagine this. It looks as if you want to hint at the existence of something like a Capitalistic second Communist International, of course an enemy one.

R – Exactly so. When I spoke of the financial International, I thought of it as of a Comintern, but having admitted the existence of the "Comintern," I would not say that they are enemies.

G – If you want to make us lose time on inventions and fantasies, I must tell you that you have chosen the wrong moment.

R – By the way, are you assuming that I am like the courtesan from the "Arabian Nights," who used her imagination at night to save her life... No, if you think that I am departing from the theme, then you are wrong. In order to reach that which we have taken as our aim I, if I am not to fail, must first of all enlighten you about the most important matters, while bearing in mind your general lack of acquaintance with that which I would call the "Higher Marxism." I dare not evade these explanations as I know well that such lack of knowledge exists in the Kremlin... Permit me to continue.

G – You may continue. But it is true that if all this were to be seen to be only a loss of time to excite the imagination, then this amusement will have a very sad epilogue. I have warned you.

R – I continue as if I have heard nothing. Insofar as you are a scholastic with relation to Capital, and I want to awaken your inductive talents, I shall remind you of some very curious things. Notice with what penetration Marx comes to conclusions given the then existence of early British industry, concerning its consequences, i.e.

the contemporary colossal industry: how he analyses it and criticizes; what a repulsive picture he gives of the manufacturer. In your imagination and that of the masses there arises the terrible picture of Capitalism in its human concretization: a fat-bellied manufacturer with a cigar in his mouth, as described by Marx, with self-satisfaction and anger throwing the wife and daughter of the worker onto the street. Is that not so? At the same time remember the moderation of Marx and his bourgeois orthodoxy when studying the question of money. In the problem of money there do not appear with him his famous contradictions. Finances do not exist for him as a thing of importance in itself; trade and the circulation of moneys are the results of the cursed system of Capitalistic production, which subjects them to itself and fully determines them. In the question of money Marx is a reactionary; to one's immense surprise he was one; bear in mind the "five-pointed star" like the Soviet one, which shines all over Europe, the star composed of the five Rothschild brothers with their banks, who possess colossal accumulations of wealth, the greatest ever known... And so this fact, so colossal that it misled the imagination of the people of that epoch, passes unnoticed with Marx. Something strange... Is that not so? It is possible that from this strange blindness of Marx there arises a phenomenon which is common to all future social revolutions. It is this: we can all confirm that when the masses take possession of a city or a country, then they always seem struck by a sort of superstitious fear of the banks and bankers. One had killed Kings, generals, bishops, policemen, priests and other representatives of the hated privileged classes; one robbed and burnt palaces, churches and even centers of science, but though the revolutions were economic-social, the lives of the bankers were respected, and as a result the magnificent buildings of the banks remained untouched... According to my information, before I had been arrested, this continues even now...

G – Where?

R – In Spain... Don't you know it? As you ask me, so tell me now: Do you not find all this very strange? Think, the police... I do not know, have you paid attention to the strange similarity which exists between the financial International and the proletarian International. I would say that one is the other side of the other, and the back side is the proletarian one as being more modern than the financial.

G – Where do you see similarity in things so opposed?

R – Objectively they are identical. As I had proved, the Comintern, paralleled, doubled by the reformist movement and the whole of syndicalism, calls forth the anarchy of production, inflation, poverty and hopelessness in the masses. Finances, chiefly the financial international, doubled, consciously or unconsciously by private finances, create the same contradictions, but in still greater numbers... Now we can already guess the reasons why Marx concealed the financial contradictions, which could not have remained hidden from his penetrating gaze, if finances had not had an ally, the influence of which – objectively revolutionary – was already then extraordinarily important.

G – An unconscious coincidence, but not an alliance which presupposes intelligence, will and agreement...

R – Let us leave this point of view if you like. Now let us better go over to the subjective analysis of finances and even more: let us see what sort of people personally are at work there. The international essence of money is well known. From this fact emerges that the organization which owns them and accumulates them is a cosmopolitan organization. Finances in their apogee – as an aim in themselves, the financial International – deny and do not recognize anything national, they do not recognize the State; and therefore it is anarchical and would be absolutely anarchical if it – the denier of any national State – were not itself, by necessity, a State in its own basic essence. The State as such is only power. And money is exclusively power.

This communistic super-state, which we are creating already during a whole century, and the scheme of which is the International of Marx. Analyze it and you will see its essence. The scheme of the International and its prototype of the USSR— that is also pure power. The basic similarity between the two creations is absolute. It is something fatalistic, inevitable, since the personalities of the authors of both was identical. The financier is just as international as the Communist. Both, with the help of differing pretexts and differing means, struggle with the national bourgeois State and deny it. Marxism in order to change it into a Communist State; from this comes that the Marxist must be an internationalist: the financier denies the bourgeois national State and his denial ends in itself; in fact he does not manifest himself as an internationalist, but as a cosmopolitan anarchist... That is his appearance at the given stage, but let us see what he really is and what he wants to be. As you see, in rejection there is a clear similarity individually between Communist-internationalists and financial-cosmopolitans; as a natural result there is the same similarity between the Communist International and the financial International...

G – This is a chance similarity subjectively and objective in contradictions, but one easily eroded and having little significance and that which is most radical and existing in reality.

R – Allow me not to reply just now, so as not to interrupt the logical sequence…I only want to decipher the basic axiom: money is power. Money is today the center of global gravity. I hope you agree with me?

G – Continue, Rakovsky, I beg of you.

R – The understanding of how the financial International has gradually, right up to our epoch, become the master of money, this magical talisman, which has become for people that which God and the nation had been formerly, is something which exceeds in scientific interest even the art of revolutionary strategy, since this is also an art and also a revolution. I shall explain it to you. Historiographers and the masses, blinded by the shouts and the pomp of the French revolution, the people, intoxicated by the fact that it had succeeded in taking all power from the King and the privileged classes, did not notice how a small group of mysterious, careful and insignificant people had taken possession of the real Royal power, the magical power, almost divine, which it obtained almost without knowing it. The masses did not notice that the power had been seized by others and that soon they had subjected them to a slavery more cruel than the King, since the latter, in view of his religious and moral prejudices, was incapable of taking advantage of such a power. So it came about that the supreme Royal power was taken over by persons, whose moral, intellectual and cosmopolitan qualities did allow them to use it. It is clear that this were people who had never been Christians, but cosmopolitans.

G – What is that for a mythical power which they had obtained?

R – They had acquired for themselves the real privilege of coining money... Do not smile, otherwise I shall have to believe that you do not know what moneys are... I ask you to put yourself in my place. My position in relation to you is that of the assistant of a doctor, who would have to explain bacteriology to a resurrected medical man of the epoch before Pasteur. But I can explain your lack of knowledge to myself and can forgive it. Our language makes use of words which provoke incorrect thoughts about things and actions, thanks to the power of the inertia of thoughts, and which do not correspond to real and exact conceptions. I say: money. It is clear that in your imagination there immediately appeared pictures of real money of metal and paper. But that is not so. Money is now not that; real circulating coin is a true anachronism. If it still exists and circulates, then it is only thanks to atavism, only because it is convenient to maintain the illusion, a purely imaginary fiction for the present day.

G – This is a brilliant paradox, risky and even poetical.

R – If you like, this is perhaps brilliant, but it is not a paradox. I know – and that is why you smiled – that States still coin money on pieces of metal or paper with Royal busts or national crests; well, so what? A great part of the money circulating, money for big affairs, as representative of all national wealth, money, yes money— it was being issued by those few people about whom I had hinted. Titles, figures, cheques, promissory notes, endorsements, discount, quotations, figures without end flooded States like a waterfall. What are in comparison with these the metallic and paper moneys?... Something devoid of influence, some kind of minimum in the face of the growing flood of the all-flooding financial money. They, being the most subtle psychologists, were able to gain even more without trouble, thanks to a lack of understanding. In addition to the immensely varied different forms of financial moneys, they created credit-money with a view to making its volume close to infinite. And to give it the speed of sound... it is an abstraction, a being of thought, a figure, number, credit, faith...

Do you understand already?... Fraud; false moneys, given a legal standing..., using other terminology, so that you should understand me. Banks, the stock exchanges and the whole world financial system— is a gigantic machine for the purpose of bringing about unnatural scandals, according to Aristotle's expression; to force money to produce money— that is something that if it is a crime in economics, then in relations to finances it is a crime against the criminal code, since it is usury. I do not know by what arguments all this is justified: by the proposition that they receive legal interest... Even accepting that, and even that admission is more than is necessary, we see that usury still exists, since even if the interest received is legal, then it invents and falsifies the non-existent capital. Banks have always by way of deposits or moneys in productive movement a certain quantity of money which is five or perhaps even a hundred times greater than there are physically coined moneys of metal or paper. I shall say nothing of those cases when the credit-moneys, i.e. false, fabricated ones, are greater than the quantity of moneys paid out as capital. Bearing in mind that lawful interest is fixed not on real capital but on non-existing capital, the interest is illegal by so many times as the fictional capital is greater than the real one.

Bear in mind that this system, which I am describing in detail, is one of the most innocent among those used for the fabrication of false money. Imagine to yourself, if you can, a small number of people, having unlimited power through the possession of real wealth, and you will see that they are the absolute dictators of the stock-exchange; and as a result of this also the dictators of production and distribution and also of work and consumption. If you have enough imagination then multiply this, by the global factor and you will see its anarchical, moral and social influence, i.e. a revolutionary one... Do you now understand?

G – No, not yet.

R – Obviously it is very difficult to understand miracles.

G – Miracle?

R – Yes, miracle. Is it not a miracle that a wooden bench has been transformed into a temple? And yet such a miracle has been seen by people a thousand times, and they did not bat an eyelid, during a whole century. Since this was an extraordinary miracle that the benches on which sat the greasy usurers to trade in their moneys, have now been converted into temples, which stand magnificently at every corner of contemporary big towns with their heathen colonnades, and crowds go there with a faith which they are already not given by heavenly gods, in order to bring assiduously their deposits of all their possessions to the god of money, who, they imagine, lives in the steel safes of the bankers, and who is preordained, thanks to his divine mission to increase the wealth to a metaphysical infinity.

G – This is the new religion of the decayed bourgeoisie?

R – Religion, yes, the religion of power.

G – You appear to be the poet of economics.

R – If you like, then in order to give a picture of finance, as of a work of art which is most obviously a work of genius and the most revolutionary of all times, poetry is required.

G – This is a faulty view. Finances, as defined by Marx, and more especially Engels, are determined by the system of Capitalistic production.

R – Exactly, but just the reverse: the Capitalistic system of production is determined by finance. The fact that Engels states the opposite and even tries to prove this, is the most obvious proof that finances rule bourgeois production. So it is and so it was even before Marx and Engels, that finances were the most powerful instrument of revolution and the Comintern was nothing but a toy in their hands. But neither Marx nor Engels will disclose or explain this. On the contrary, making use of their talent as scientists, they had to camouflage truth for a second time in the interests of the revolution. And that both of them did.

G – This story is not new. All this somewhat reminds me of what Trotsky had written some ten years ago.

R – Tell me...

G – When he says that the Comintern is a conservative organization in comparison with the stock-exchange in New York; he points at the big bankers as being the inventors of the revolution.

R – Yes, he said this in a small book in which he foretold the fall of England... Yes, he said this and added: "Who pushes England along the path of revolution?"... and replied: "Not Moscow, but New York."

G – But remember also his assertion that if the financiers of New York had forged the revolution, then it was done unconsciously.

R – The explanation which I had already given in order to help to understand why Engels and Marx camouflaged the truth, is equally applicable also to Leo Trotsky.

G – I value in Trotsky only that he in a sort of literary form interpreted an opinion of a fact which as such was too well known, with which one had already reckoned previously. Trotsky himself states quite correctly that these bankers "carry out irresistibly and unconsciously their revolutionary mission."

R – And they carry out their mission despite the fact that Trotsky has declared it? What a strange thing! Why do they not improve their actions?

G – The financiers are unconscious revolutionaries since they are such only objectively, as the result of their intellectual incapacity of seeing the final consequences.

R – You believe this sincerely? You think that among these real geniuses there are some who are unconscious? You consider to be idiots people to whom today the whole world is subjected? This would really be a very stupid contradiction!

G – What do you pretend to?

R – I simply assert that they are revolutionaries objectively and subjectively, quite consciously.

G – The bankers! You must be mad?

R – I, no... But you? Think a little. These people are just like you and me. The circumstance that they control moneys in unlimited amounts, insofar as they themselves create them, does not give us the opportunity of determining the limits of all their ambitions... If there is something which provides a man with full satisfaction then it is the satisfaction of his ambition. And most of all the satisfaction of his will to power. Why should not these people, the bankers, have the impulse towards power, towards full power? Just as it happens to you and to me.

G – But if, according to you – and I think the same – they already have global political power, then what other power do they want to possess?

R – I have already told you: Full power. Such power as Stalin has in the USSR, but world-wide.

G – Such power as Stalin's, but with the opposite aim.

R – Power, if in reality it is absolute, can be only one. The idea of the absolute excludes multiplicity. For that reason the power sought by the Comintern and "Comintern," which are things of the same order, being absolute, must also in politics be unique and identical: Absolute power has a purpose in itself, otherwise it is not absolute. And until the present day there has not yet been invented another machine of total power except the Communist State. Capitalistic bourgeois power, even on its highest rung of the ladder, the power of Caesar, is limited power since if, in theory, it was the personification of the deity in the Pharaohs and Caesars in ancient times, then nevertheless, thanks to the economic character of life in those primitive States and owing to the technical under-development of the State apparatus, there was always room for individual freedom. Do you understand that those who already partially rule over nations and worldly governments have pretensions to absolute domination? Understand that that is the only thing which they have not yet reached.

G – This is interesting: at least as an example of insanity.

R – Certainly, insanity in a lesser degree than in the case of Lenin, who dreamt of power over the whole world in his attic in Switzerland or the insanity of Stalin, dreaming of the same thing during his exile in a Siberian hut. I think that dreams of such ambitions are much more natural for the moneyed people, living in the skyscrapers of New York.

G – Let us conclude: Who are they?

R – You are so naive that you think that if I knew who "They" are, I would be here as a prisoner?

G – Why?

R – For a very simple reason, since he who is acquainted with them would not be put into a position in which he would be obliged to report on them… This is an elementary rule of every intelligent conspiracy, which you must well understand.

G – But you said that they are the bankers?

R – Not I; remember that I always spoke of the financial International, and when mentioning persons I said "They" and nothing more. If you want that I should inform you openly then I shall only give facts, but not names, since I do not know them. I think I shall not be wrong if I tell you that not one of "Them" is a person who occupies a political position or a position in the World Bank. As I understood after the murder of Rathenau in Rapallo, they give political or financial positions only to intermediaries. Obviously to persons who are trustworthy and loyal, which can be guaranteed a thousand ways: thus one can assert that bankers and politicians— are only men of straw… even though they occupy very high places and are made to appear to be the authors of the plans which are carried out.

G – Although all this can be understood and is also logical, but is not your declaration of not knowing only an evasion? As it seems to me, and according to the information I have, you occupied a sufficiently high place in this conspiracy to have known much more. You do not even know a single one of them personally?

R – Yes, but of course you do not believe me. I have come to that moment where I had explained that I am talking about a person and persons with a personality... how should one say?... a mystical one, like Gandhi or something like that, but without any external display. Mystics of pure power, who have become free from all vulgar trifles. I do not know if you understand me? Well, as to their place of residence and names, I do not know them... Imagine Stalin just now, in reality ruling the USSR, but not surrounded by stone walls, not having any personnel around him, and having the same guarantees for his life as any other citizen. By which means could he guard against attempts on his life? He is first of all a conspirator, however great his power, he is anonymous.

G – What you are saying is logical, but I do not believe you.

R – But still believe me; I know nothing; if I knew then how happy I would be! I would not be here, defending my life. I well understand your doubts and that, in view of your police education, you feel the need for some knowledge about persons. To honor you and also because this is essential for the aim which we both have set ourselves, I shall do all I can in order to inform you. You know that according to the unwritten history known only to us, the founder of the First Communist International is indicated, of course secretly, as being Weishaupt. You remember his name? He was the head of the masonry which is known by the name of the Illuminati; this name he borrowed from the second anti-Christian conspiracy of that era— Gnosticism. This important revolutionary, Semite and former Jesuit, foreseeing the triumph of the French revolution decided, or perhaps he was ordered (some mention as his chief the important philosopher Mendelssohn) to found a secret organization which was to provoke and push the French revolution to go further than its political objectives, with the aim of transforming it into a social revolution for the establishment of Communism. In those heroic times it was colossally dangerous to mention Communism as an aim; from this derive the various precautions and secrets, which had to surround the Illuminati. More than a hundred years were required before a man could confess to being a Communist without danger of going to prison or being executed. This is more or less known. What is not known are the relations between Weishaupt and his followers with the first of the Rothschilds. The secret of the acquisition of wealth of the best known bankers could have been explained by the fact that they were the treasurers of this first Comintern. There is evidence that when the five brothers spread out to the five provinces of the financial empire of Europe, they had some secret help for the accumulation of these enormous sums: it is possible that they were those first Communists from the Bavarian catacombs who were already spread all over Europe. But others say, and I think with better reason, that the Rothschilds were not the treasurers, but the Marx and the highest chiefs of the First International – already the open one – and among them Herzen and Heine, were controlled by Baron Lionel Rothschild, whose revolutionary portrait was done by Disraeli [in Coningsby —Transl.] the English Premier, who was his creature, and has been left to us. He described him in the character of Sidonia, a man, who, according to the story, was a multi-millionaire, knew and controlled spies, carbonari, freemasons, secret Jews, gypsies, revolutionaries etc., etc. All this seems fantastic. But it has been proved that Sidonia is an idealized portrait of the son of Nathan Rothschild, which can also be deduced from that campaign which he raised against

Tsar Nicholas in favor of Herzen. He won this campaign. If all that which we can guess in the light of these facts is true, then, I think, we could even determine who invented this terrible machine of accumulation and anarchy, which is the financial International. At the same time, I think, he would be the same person who also created the revolutionary International. It is an act of genius: to create with the help of Capitalism accumulation of the highest degree, to push the proletariat towards strikes, to sow hopelessness, and at the same time to create an organization which must unite the proletarians with the purpose of driving them into revolution. This is to write the most majestic chapter of history. Even more: remember the phrase of the mother of the five Rothschild brothers: "If my sons want it, then there will be no war." This means that they were the arbiters, the masters of peace and war, but not emperors. Are you capable of visualizing the fact of such a cosmic importance? Is not war already a revolutionary function? War— the Commune. Since that time every war was a giant step towards Communism. As if some mysterious force satisfied the passionate wish of Lenin, which he had expressed to Gorky. Remember: 1905-1914. Do admit at least that two of the three levers of power which lead to Communism are not controlled and cannot be controlled by the proletariat. Wars were not brought about and were not controlled by either the Third International or the USSR, which did not yet exist at that time. Equally they cannot be provoked and still less controlled by those small groups of Bolsheviks who plod along in the emigration, although they want war. This is quite obvious. The International and the USSR have even fewer possibilities for such immense accumulations of capital and the creation of national or international anarchy in Capitalistic production. Such an anarchy which is capable of forcing people to burn huge quantities of foodstuffs, rather than give them to starving people, and is capable of that which Rathenau described in one of his phrases, i.e.: "To bring about that half the world will fabricate dung, and the other half will use it." And, after all, can the proletariat believe that it is the cause of this inflation, growing in geometric progression, this devaluation, the constant acquisition of surplus values and the accumulation of financial capital, but not usury capital, and that as the result of the fact that it cannot prevent the constant lowering of its purchasing power, there takes place the proletarization of the middle classes, who are the true opponents of revolution? The proletariat does not control the lever of economics or the lever of war. But it is itself the third lever, the only visible and demonstrable lever, which carries out the final blow at the power of the Capitalistic State and takes it over. Yes, they seize it, if "They" yield it to them…

G – I again repeat to you that all this, which you have set out in such a literate form, has a name which we have already repeated to excess in this endless conversation: the natural contradictions of Capitalism and if, as you claim, there is yet someone else's will and activity apart from the proletariat, then I want you to indicate to me concretely a personal case.

R – You require only one? Well, then listen to a small story: "They" isolated the Tsar diplomatically for the Russo-Japanese War, and the United States financed Japan; speaking precisely, this was done by Jacob Schiff, the head of the bank of Kuhn, Loeb & Co., which is the successor of the House of Rothschild, whence Schiff originated. He had such power that he achieved that States which had colonial possessions in Asia supported the creation of the Japanese Empire which was inclined towards xenophobia; and Europe already feels the effects of this xenophobia. From the prisoner-of-war camps there came to Petrograd the best fighters, trained as revolutionary agents; they were sent there from America with the permission of Japan, obtained through the persons who had financed it. The Russo-Japanese War, thanks to the organized defeat of the Tsar's army, called forth the revolution of 1905, which, though it was premature, but was very nearly successful; even if it did not win, it still created the required political conditions for the victory of 1917. I shall say even more. Have you read the biography of Trotsky? Recall its first revolutionary period. He is still quite a young man; after his flight from Siberia he lived some time among the émigrés in London, Paris, and Switzerland; Lenin, Plekhanov, Martov and other chiefs look on him only as a promising newcomer. But he already dares during the first split to behave independently, trying to become the arbiter of the reunion. In 1905 he is 25 years old and he returns to Russia alone, without a party and without his own organization. Read the reports of the revolution of 1905 which have not been "pruned" by Stalin; for example that of Lunatcharsky, who was not a Trotskyite. Trotsky is the chief figure during the revolution in Petrograd. This is how it really was. Only he emerges from it with increased popularity and influence. Neither Lenin, nor Martov, nor Plekhanov acquire popularity. They only keep it and even lose a little. How and why there rises the unknown Trotsky, gaining power by one move greater than that which the oldest and most influential revolutionaries had? Very simple: he marries. Together with him there arrives in Russia his wife— Sedova. Do you know who she is? She is associated with Zhivotovsky, linked with the bankers Warburg, partners and relatives of Jacob Schiff, i.e. of that financial group which, as I had said, had also financed the revolution of 1905. Here is the reason why Trotsky, in one move, moves to the top of the revolutionary list. And here, too, you have the key to his real personality. Let us jump to 1914. Behind the back of the people who made the attempt on the Archduke there stands Trotsky, and that attempt provoked the European War. Do you really believe that the murder and the war— are simple coincidences?..., as had been said at one of the Zionist congresses by Lord Melchett. Analyze in the light of "non-coincidence" the development of the military actions in Russia. "Defeatism" is an exemplary word. The help of the Allies for the Tsar was regulated and controlled with such skill that it gave the Allied ambassadors the right to make an argument of this and to get from Nicholas, thanks to his stupidity, suicidal advances, one after another. The mass of the Russian cannon fodder was immense, but not inexhaustible. A series of organized defeats led to the revolution. When the threat came from all sides, then a cure was found in the form of the establishment of a democratic republic— an "ambassadorial republic" as Lenin called it i.e. this meant the elimination of any threat to the revolutionaries. But that is not yet all. Kerensky was to provoke the future advance at the cost of a very great deal of blood. He brings it about so that the democratic revolution should spread beyond its bounds. And even still more: Kerensky was to surrender the State fully to Communism, and he does it. Trotsky has the chance in an "unnoticed manner" to occupy the whole State apparatus. What a strange blindness! Well that is the reality of the much praised October revolution. The Bolsheviks took that which "They" gave them.

G – You dare to say that Kerensky was a collaborator of Lenin?

R – Of Lenin— no. Of Trotsky— yes; it is more correct to say— a collaborator of "Them."

G – An absurdity!

R – You cannot understand… precisely you? It surprises me. If you were to be a spy and, while hiding your identity, you were to attain the position of commander of the enemy fortress, then would you not open the gates to the attacking forces in whose service you actually were? You would not have become a prisoner who had experienced defeat? Would you not have been in danger of death during the attack on the fortress if one of the attackers, not knowing that your uniform is only a mask, would have taken you for an enemy? Believe me: despite the statues and mausoleum— Communism is indebted to Kerensky much more than to Lenin.

G – You want to say that Kerensky was a conscious and voluntary defeatist?

R – Yes to me that is quite clear. Understand that I personally took part in all this. I shall tell you even more: Do you know who financed the October revolution? "They" financed it, in particular through those same bankers who had financed Japan in 1905, i.e. Jacob Schiff, and the brothers Warburg; that means through the great banking constellation, through one of the five banks who are members of the Federal Reserve, through the bank of Kuhn, Loeb & Co., here there took part also other American and European bankers, such as Guggenheim, Hanauer, Breitung, Aschberg, the "Nya Banken" of Stockholm. I was there "by chance," there in Stockholm, and participated in the transmission of funds. Until Trotsky arrived I was the only person who was an intermediary from the revolutionary side. But at last Trotsky came; I must underline that the Allies had expelled him from France for being a defeatist. And the same Allies released him so that he could be a defeatist in allied Russia… "Another chance." Who arranged it? The same people who had succeeded that Lenin passed through Germany. Yes, "They" were able to get the defeatist Trotsky out of a Canadian camp to England and send him on to Russia, giving him the chance to pass freely through all the Allied controls; others of "Them" – a certain Rathenau – accomplishes the journey of Lenin through enemy Germany. If you will undertake the study of the history of the revolution and civil war without prejudices, and will use all your enquiring capabilities, which you know how to apply to things much less important and less obvious, then when you study informations in their totality, and also study separate details right up to anecdotal happenings you will meet with a whole series of "amazing chances."

G – Alright, let us accept the hypothesis that not everything was simply a matter of luck. What deductions do you make here for practical results?

R – Let me finish this little story, and then we shall both arrive at conclusions. From the time of his arrival in Petrograd Trotsky was openly received by Lenin. As you know sufficiently well, during the interval between the two revolutions there had been deep differences between them. All is forgotten and Trotsky emerges as the master of his trade in the matter of the triumph of the revolution, whether Stalin wants this or not. Why? This secret is known to the wife of Lenin— Krupskaya. She knows who Trotsky is in fact; it is she who persuaded Lenin to receive Trotsky. If he had not received him, then Lenin would have remained blocked up in Switzerland; this alone had been for him a serious reason, and in addition he knew that Trotsky provided money and helped to get a colossal international assistance, a proof of this was the sealed train. Furthermore it was the result of Trotsky's work, and not of the iron determination of Lenin that there was the unification round the insignificant party of the Bolsheviks of the whole Left-wing revolutionary camp, the social-revolutionaries and the anarchists. It was not for nothing that the real party of the "non-party" Trotsky was the ancient "Bund" of the Jewish proletariat, from which emerged all the Moscow revolutionary branches, and to whom it gave 90% of its leaders; not the official and well-known Bund, but the secret Bund which had been infiltrated into all the Socialist parties, the leaders of which were almost all under its control.

G – And Kerensky too?

R – Kerensky too..., and also some other leaders who were not Socialists, the leaders of the bourgeois political fractions.

G – How is that?

R – You forget about the role of freemasonry in the first phase of the democratic-bourgeois revolution?

G – Were they also controlled by the Bund?

R – Naturally, as the nearest step, but in fact subject to "Them."

G – Despite the rising tide of Marxism which also threatened their lives and privileges?

R – Despite all that; obviously they did not see that danger. Bear in mind that every mason saw and hoped to see in his imagination more that there was in reality, because he imagined that which was profitable for him. As a proof of the political power of their association they saw that masons were in governments and at the pinnacle of the States of the bourgeois nations, while their numbers were growing all the time. Bear in mind that at that time the rulers of all the Allied nations were freemasons, with very few exceptions. This was to them an argument of great force. They fully believed that the revolution would stop at the bourgeois republic of the French type.

G – In accordance with the picture which was given of the Russia of 1917 one had to be a very naive person to believe all this...

R – They were and are such. Masons had learned nothing from that first lesson which, for them, had been the Great Revolution, in which they played a colossal revolutionary role; it consumed the majority of masons, beginning with the Grand Master of the Orleans Lodge, more correctly the freemason Louis XVI, in order then to continue to destroy the Girondistes, the Hebertistes, the Jacoboins etc..... and if some survived it was due to the month of Brumaire.

G – Do you want to say that the freemasons have to die at the hands of the revolution which has been brought about with their cooperation?

R – Exactly so. You have formulated a truth which is veiled by a great secret. I am a mason, you already knew about that. Is that not so? Well, I shall tell you this great secret, which they promise to disclose to a mason in one of the higher degrees, but which is not disclosed to him either in the 25th, nor the 33rd, nor the 93rd, nor any other high level of any ritual. It is clear that I know of this not as a freemason, but as one who belongs to "Them"...

G – And what is it?

R – Every Masonic organization tries to attain and to create all the required prerequisites for the triumph of the Communist revolution; this is the obvious aim of freemasonry; it is clear that all this is done under various pretexts; but they always conceal themselves behind their well-known treble slogan. (Liberty, Equality, Fraternity—Transl.) You understand? But since the Communist revolution has in mind the liquidation, as a class, of the whole bourgeoisie, the physical destruction of all bourgeois political rulers, it follows that the real secret of masonry is the suicide of freemasonry as an organization, and the physical suicide of every more important mason. You can, of course, understand that such an end, which is being prepared for every mason, fully deserves the secrecy, decorativeness and the inclusion of yet another whole series of secrets, with a view to concealing the real one. If one day you were to be present at some future revolution then do not miss the opportunity of observing the gestures of surprise and the expression of stupidity on the face of some freemason at the moment when he realizes that he must die at the hands of the revolutionaries. How he screams and wants that one should value his services to the revolution! It is a sight at which one can die... but of laughter.

G – And you still deny the inborn stupidity of the bourgeoisie?

R – I deny it in the bourgeoisie as a class, but not in certain sectors. The existence of madhouses does not prove universal madness. Freemasonry is also a madhouse, but at liberty. But I continue further: the revolution has been victorious, the seizure of power has been achieved. There arises the first problem, peace, and with it the first differences within the party, in which there participate the forces of the coalition, which takes advantage of power. I shall not explain to you that which is well known about the struggle which developed in Moscow between the adherents and opponents of the peace of Brest-Litovsk. I shall only point out to you that which had already become evident then and was later called the Trotskyist opposition, i.e. these are the people, a part of whom have already been liquidated and the other part is to be liquidated: they were all against the signing of the peace treaty. That peace was a mistake and an unconscious betrayal by Lenin of the International Revolution. Imagine to yourself the Bolsheviks in Versailles at the Peace Conference, and then in the League of Nations, finding themselves inside Germany with the Red Army, which had been armed and increased by the Allies. The Soviet State should have participated with arms in the German revolution… Quite another map of Europe would then have emerged. But Lenin, intoxicated with power, with the help of Stalin, who had also tasted the fruits of power supported by the national Russian wing of the party, having at their disposal the material resources, enforced their will. Then was born "Socialism in one country," i.e. National-Communism, which has today reached its apogee under Stalin. It is obvious that there was a struggle, but only in such a form and extent that the Communist State should not be destroyed; this condition was binding on the opposition during the whole time of its further struggle right up to the present day. This was the reason for our first failure and all those which followed. But the fight was severe, cruel, although concealed in order not to compromise our participation in power. Trotsky organized, with the help of his friends, the attempt on Lenin's life by Kaplan. On his orders Blumkin killed the ambassador Mirbach. The coup d'etat which was prepared by Spiridonova with her social-revolutionaries had been coordinated with Trotsky. His man for all these affairs, who was immune from all suspicions, was that Rosenblum, a Lithuanian Jew, who used the name of O'Reilly, and was known as the best spy of the British Intelligence. In fact he was a man from "Them." The reason why this famous Rosenblum was chosen, who was known only as a British spy, was that in case of failure the responsibility for assassinations and conspiracies would fall not on Trotsky, and not on us, but on England. So it happened. Thanks to the Civil War we rejected conspiratorial and terrorist methods as we were given the chance of having in our hands the real forces of the State, insofar as Trotsky became the organizer and chief of the Soviet Army; before that the army had continuously retreated before the Whites and the territory of the USSR was reduced to the size of the former Moscow Principality. But here, as if by magic, it begins to win. What do you think, why? As the result of magic or chance? I shall tell you: when Trotsky took over the top command of the Red Army then he had by this in his hands the forces necessary to seize power. A series of victories was to increase his prestige and forces: it was already possible to defeat the Whites. Do you think that that official history was true which ascribes to the unarmed and ill-disciplined Red Army the fact that with its help there was achieved a series of victories?

G – But to whom then?

R – To the extent of ninety per cent they were indebted to "Them." You must not forget that the Whites were, in their way, democratic. The Mensheviks were with them and the remnants of all the old Liberal parties. Inside these forces "They" always had in their service many people, consciously and unconsciously. When Trotsky began to command then these people were ordered systematically to betray the Whites and at the same time they were promised participation, in a more or less short time, in the Soviet Government. Maisky was one of those people, one of the few in the case of which this promise was carried out, but he was able to achieve this only after Stalin had become convinced of his loyalty. This sabotage, linked with a progressive diminution of the help of the Allies to the White generals, who apart from all that were luckless idiots, forced them to experience defeat after defeat. Finally Wilson introduced in his famous 14 Points Point 6,* the existence of which was enough in order to bring to an end once and for all the attempts of the Whites to fight against the USSR. The Civil War strengthens the position of Trotsky as the heir of Lenin. So it was without any doubt. The old revolutionary could now die, having acquired fame. If he remained alive after the bullet of Kaplan, he did not emerge alive after the secret process of the forcible ending of his life, to which he was subjected.

G – Trotsky shortened his life? This is a big favorable point for our trial! Was it not Levin who was Lenin's doctor?

R – Trotsky?... It is probable that he participated, but it is quite certain that he knew about it. But as far as the technical realization is concerned..., that is unimportant; who knows this? "They" have a sufficient number of channels in order to penetrate to wherever they want.

G – In any event the murder of Lenin is a matter of the greatest importance and it would be worthwhile to transfer it for examination to the next trial... What do you think, Rakovsky, if you were by chance to be the author of this affair? It is clear that if you fail to achieve success in this conversation... The technical execution suits you well as a doctor...

R – I do not recommend this to you. Leave this matter alone, it is sufficiently dangerous for Stalin himself. You will be able to spread your propaganda as you wish; but "They" have their propaganda which is more powerful and the question as to *qui podest*— who gains, will force one to see in Stalin the murderer of Lenin, and that argument will be stronger than any confessions extracted from Levin, me or anyone else.

G – What do you want to say by this?

R – That it is the classical and infallible rule in the determination of who the murderer is to check who gained..., and as far as the assassination of Lenin is concerned, in this case the beneficiary was his chief— Stalin. Think about this and I very much ask you not to make these remarks, as they distract me and do not make it possible for me to finish.

G – Very well, continue, but you already know...

R – It is well known that if Trotsky did not inherit from Lenin then it was not because by human calculations there was something missing in the plan. During Lenin's illness Trotsky held in his hands all the threads of power, which were more than sufficient to enable him to succeed Lenin. And measures had been taken to declare a sentence of death on Stalin. For Trotsky the dictator it was enough to have

---

* Wilson's Point 6 read: "The evacuation of all Russian territory, and such a settlement of all questions affecting Russia as will secure the best and freest co-operation of the other nations of the world in obtaining for her an unhampered and unembarrassed opportunity for the independent determination of her own political development and national policy, and assure her of a sincere welcome into the society of free nations under institutions of her own choosing, and more than a welcome, assistance also of every kind that she may need and may herself desire. The treatment accorded Russia by her sister nations in the months to come will be the acid test of their good will, of heir comprehension of her needs as distinguished from their own interests, and of their intelligent and unselfish sympathy." —Transl.

in his hands the letter of Lenin against his then chief— Stalin, which had been torn from her husband by Krupskaya, to liquidate Stalin.* But a stupid mischance, as you know, ruined all our chances. Trotsky became ill unexpectedly and at the decisive moment, when Lenin dies, he becomes incapable of any action during a period of several months. Despite his possession of enormous advantages, the obstacle was our organization of the affair, i.e. its personal centralization. It is obvious that such a person as Trotsky, prepared in advance for his mission, which he was to realize, cannot be created at once, by improvisation. None among us, not even Zinoviev, had the requisite training and qualities for this undertaking; on the other hand Trotsky, being afraid of being displaced, did not himself want to help anybody. Thus, after the death of Lenin, when we had to be face to face with Stalin, who commenced a feverish activity, we foresaw then already our defeat in the Central Committee. We had to improvise a decision: and it was to ally ourselves with Stalin, to become Stalinists more than he himself, to exaggerate in everything and, therefore, to sabotage. The rest you know already: that was our uninterrupted subterranean struggle and our continuous failure to Stalin's advantage, while he displays police talents of genius, having absolutely no equals in the past. And even more: Stalin, possessing national atavism, which had not been uprooted in him by his early Marxism, apparently for that reason underlines his pan-Russianism, and in this connexion resurrects a class which we had to destroy, that is the class of National-Communists, as opposed to the Internationalist-Communists, which we are. He places the International at the service of the USSR and it already accepts his mastery. If we want to find an historical parallel, then we must point to Bonapartism, and if we want to find a person of Stalin's type, then we shall not find an historical parallel for him. But perhaps I shall be able to find it in its basic characteristics by combining two people: Fouche and Napoleon. Let us try to deprive the latter of his second half, his accessories, uniforms, military rank, crown and such like things, which, it seems, do not tempt Stalin, and then together they will give us a type identical with Stalin in the most important respects: he is the killer of the revolution, he does not serve it, but makes use of its services; he represents the most ancient Russian Imperialism, just as Napoleon identified himself with the Gauls, he created an aristocracy, even if not a military one, one, since there are no victories, then a bureaucratic-police one.

G – That is enough. Rakovsky. You are not here to make Trotskyist propaganda. Will you at last get to something concrete?

R – It is clear that I shall, but not before I had reached the point at which you will have formulated for yourself an at least superficial conception concerning "Them," with whom you will have to reckon in practice and in concrete actuality. Not sooner. For me it is far more important than for you not to fail, which you must, naturally, understand.

G – Well, try to shorten the story as far as possible.

R – Our failures, which get worse every year, prevent the immediate carrying out of that which "They" have prepared in the after-war period for the further leap of the

---

* It will be observed that twice Rakovsky states that Stalin had been Lenin's chief; this may be a misunderstanding —Transl.

revolution forward. The Versailles Treaty, quite inexplicable for the politicians and economists of all nations, insofar as nobody could guess its projection, was the most decisive precondition for the revolution.

G – This is a very curious theory. How do you explain it?

R – The Versailles reparations and economic limitations were not determined by the advantages of individual nations. Their arithmetical absurdity was so obvious that even the most outstanding economists of the victorious countries soon exposed this. France alone demanded as reparations a great deal more than the cost of all her national possessions, more than one would have had to pay if the whole of France had been converted into a Sahara; even worse was the decision to impose on Germany payment obligations which were many times greater that it could pay, even if it had sold itself fully and given over the whole of its national production. In the end the true result was that in practice Germany was forced to carry out a fantastic dumping so that it could pay something on account of reparations. And of what did the dumping consist? An insufficiency of consumer goods, hunger in Germany and in corresponding measure unemployment in the importing countries. And since they could not import there was also unemployment in Germany. Hunger and unemployment on both sides; all this were the first results of Versailles… Was this treaty revolutionary or not? Even more was done: one undertook an equal control in the international plane. Do you know what that undertaking represents in the revolutionary plane? It means to impose an anarchical absurdity to force every national economy to produce in sufficient volume all that it needs, while assuming that to attain that one does not have to take account of climate, natural riches and also the technical education of directors and workers. The means for compensation for inborn inequalities of soil, climate, availability of minerals, oil, etc., etc. in various national economies, were always the circumstance that poor countries had to work more. This means that they had to exploit more deeply the capacities of the working force in order to lessen the difference which arises from the poverty of the soil; and to this are added a number of other inequalities which had to be compensated by similar measures, let us take the example of industrial equipment. I shall not expand the problem further, but the control of the working day carried through by the League of Nations on the basis of an abstract principle of the equality of the working day, was a reality in the context of an unchanged International Capitalist system of production and exchange and established economic inequality, since here we had to deal with an indifference to the aim of work, which is a sufficient production. The immediate result of this was an insufficiency of production, compensated by imports from countries with a sufficient natural economy and an industrial self-sufficiency: insofar as Europe had gold, that import was paid by gold. Then came the apparent boom in America which exchanged its immense production for gold and gold certificates, of which there was plenty. On the model of any anarchy of production there appeared at that period an unheard-of financial anarchy. "They" took advantage of it on the pretext of helping it with the aid of another and still greater anarchy: the inflation of the official money (cash) and the a hundred times greater inflation of their own money, credit money, i.e. false money. Remember how systematically there came devaluation in many countries; the destruction of the value of money in Germany, the American crisis and its phenomenal consequences ……, a record unemployment; more than thirty million unemployed in Europe and USA alone. Well, did not the Versailles Peace Treaty and its League of Nations serve as a revolutionary pre-condition?

G – This could have happened even if not intended. Could you not prove to me why the revolution and Communism retreat before logical deductions; and more than that: they oppose fascism which has conquered in Spain and Germany... What can you tell me?

R – I shall tell you that only in the case of the non-recognition of "Them" and their aims you would be right..., but you must not forget about their existence and aims, and also the fact that in the USSR power is in the hands of Stalin.

G – I do not see the connection here....

R – Because you do not want to: you have more than sufficient deductive talents and capabilities of reasoning. I repeat again: for us Stalin is not a Communist, but a Bonapartist.

G – So what?

R – We do not wish that the great preconditions which we had created at Versailles for the triumph of the Communist revolution in the world, which, as you see, have become a gigantic reality, would serve the purpose of bringing victory to Stalin's Bonapartism... Is that sufficiently clear for you? Everything would have been different if in this case Trotsky had been the dictator of the USSR; that would have meant that "They" would have been the chiefs of International Communism.

G – But surely fascism is totally anti-Communist, as in relation to the Trotskyist and the Stalinist Communism... and if the power which you ascribe to "Them" is so great, how is it that they were unable to avoid this?

R – Because it were precisely "They" who gave Hitler the possibility of triumphing.

G – You exceed all the boundaries of absurdity.

R – The absurd and the miraculous become mixed as the result of a lack of culture. Listen to me. I have already admitted the defeat of the opposition. "They" saw in the end that Stalin cannot be overthrown by a coup d'etat and their historical experience suggested to them the decision of a repetition (repris) with Stalin of that which had been done with the Tsar. There was here one difficulty, which seemed to us insuperable. In the whole of Europe there was not a single aggressor-State. Not one of them was geographically well placed and had an army sufficient for an attack on Russia. If there was no such country, then "They" had to create it. Only Germany had the corresponding population and positions suitable for an attack on the USSR, and it was capable of defeating Stalin; you can understand that the Weimar republic had not been invented as an aggressor either politically or economically; on the contrary, it was suited to an invasion. On the horizon of a hungry Germany there sparkled the meteor of Hitler. A pair of penetrating eyes fixed their attention on it. The world was the witness to his lightning rise. I shall not say that all of it was the work of our hands, no. His rise, uninterruptedly increasing in extent, took place as the result of the Revolutionary-Communist economy of Versailles. Versailles had had in mind not the creation of preconditions for the triumph of Hitler, but for the proletarization of Germany, for unemployment and hunger, as the result of which there should have triumphed the Communist revolution. But insofar as, thanks to the existence of Stalin at the head of the USSR and the International, the latter did not succeed, and as a result of an unwillingness to give up Germany to Bonapartism, these preconditions were somewhat abated in the Davis and Young Plans, in expectation that meanwhile the opposition would come to power in Russia..., but that, too, did not happen; but the existence of revolutionary preconditions had to produce its results. The economic predetermination of Germany would have forced the proletariat into revolutionary actions. Through the fault of Stalin the Social-International revolution had to be held up and the German proletariat sought inclusion in the National-Socialist revolution. This was dialectical, but given all the preconditions and according to common sense the National-Socialist revolution could never have triumphed there. That was not yet all. It was necessary that the Trotskyists and Socialists should divide the masses with an already awakened and whole class consciousness— in accordance with instructions. With this business we concerned ourselves. But even more was needed: In 1929, when the National-Socialist Party began to experience a crisis of growth and it had insufficient financial resources, "They" sent their ambassador there. I even know his name: it was one of the Warburgs. In direct negotiations with Hitler they agreed as to the financing of the National-Socialist Party, and the latter received in a couple of years millions of Dollars, sent to it from Wall Street, and millions of Marks from German financiers through Schacht; the upkeep of the S.A. and S.S. and also the financing of the elections which took place, which gave Hitler power, are done on the Dollars and Marks sent by "Them."

G – Those who, according to you, want to achieve full Communism, arm Hitler, who swears that he will uproot the first Communist nation. This, if one is to believe you, is something very logical for the financiers.

R – You again forget the Stalinist Bonapartism. Remember that against Napoleon, the strangler of the French revolution, who stole its strength, there stood the objective revolutionaries— Louis XVIII, Wellington, Metternich and right up to the Tsar- Autocrat... This is 22 carat, according to the strict Stalinist doctrine. You must know by heart his theses about colonies with regard to imperialistic countries. Yes, according to him the Kings of Afghanistan and Egypt are objectively Communists owing to their struggle against His Britannic Majesty; why cannot Hitler be objectively Communist since he is fighting against the autocratic "Tsar Koba I"? (Meaning Stalin —Transl.) After all there is Hitler with his growing military power, and he already extends the boundaries of the Third Reich, and in future will do more... to such an extent as to have enough strength and possibilities to attack and fully destroy Stalin... Do you not observe the general sympathy of the Versailles wolves, who limit themselves only to a weak growl? Is this yet another chance, accident? Hitler will invade the USSR and as in 1917, when defeat suffered by the Tsar then gave us the opportunity of overthrowing him, so the defeat of Stalin will help us to remove him... Again the hour of the world revolution will strike. Since the democratic states, at present put to sleep, will help to bring about the general change at that moment, when Trotsky will take power into his hands, as during the Civil War. Hitler will attack from the West, his generals will rise and liquidate him... Now tell me, was not Hitler objectively a Communist? Yes or no?

G – I do not believe in fairy tales or miracles...

R – Well if you do not want to believe that "They" are able to achieve that which they had already achieved, then prepare to observe an invasion of the USSR and the liquidation of Stalin within a year. You think this is a miracle or an accident, well then prepare to see and experience that... But are you really able to refuse to believe that of which I have spoken, though this is still only a hypothesis? You will begin to act in this direction only at that moment when you will begin to see the proofs in the light of my talk.

G – All right, let us talk in the form of a supposition. What will you say?

R – You yourself had drawn attention to the coincidence of opinions, which took place between us. We are not at the moment interested in the attack on the USSR, since the fall of Stalin would presuppose the destruction of Communism, the existence of which interests us despite the circumstance that it is formal, as that gives us the certainty that we shall succeed in taking it over and then converting it into real Communism. I think that I have given you the position at the moment quite accurately.

G – Splendid, the solution...

R – First of all we must make sure that there would be no potential possibility of an attack by Hitler.

G – If, as you confirm, it were "They" who made him Fuhrer, then they have power over him and he must obey them.

R – Owing to the fact that I was in a hurry I did not express myself quite correctly and you did not understand me well. If it is true that "They" financed Hitler, then that does not mean that they disclosed to him their existence and their aims. The ambassador Warburg presented himself under a false name and Hitler did not even guess his race, he also lied regarding whose representative he was. He told him that he had been sent by the financial circles of Wall Street who were interested in financing the National-Socialist movement with the aim of creating a threat to France, whose governments pursue a financial policy which provokes a crisis in the USA.

G – And Hitler believed it?

R – We do not know. That was not so important, whether he did or did not believe our explanations; our aim was to provoke a war..., and Hitler was war. Do you now understand?

G – I understand. Consequently I do not see any other way of stopping him as the creation of a coalition of the USSR with the democratic nations, which would be capable of frightening Hitler. I think he will not be able to attack simultaneously all the countries of the world. The most would be— each in turn.

R – Does not a simpler solution come to your mind..., I would say— a counter-revolutionary one?

G – To avoid war against the USSR?

R – Shorten the phrase by half... and repeat with me "avoid war"... is that not an absolutely counter-revolutionary thing? Every sincere Communist imitating his idol Lenin and the greatest revolutionary strategists must always wish for war. Nothing is so effective in bringing nearer the victory of revolution as war. This is a Marxist-Leninist dogma, which you must preach. Now further: Stalin's National-Communism, this type of Bonapartism, is capable of blinding the intellect of the most pure-blooded Communists, right up to the point at which it prevents their seeing that the transformation into which Stalin has fallen, i.e., that he subjects the revolution to the State, and not the State to the revolution, it would be correct...

G – Your hate of Stalin blinds you and you contradict yourself. Have we not agreed that an attack on the USSR would not be welcome?

R – But why should war be necessarily against the Soviet Union?

G – But on what other country could Hitler make war? It is sufficiently clear that he would direct his attack on the USSR, of this he speaks in his speeches. What further proofs do you need?

R – If you, the people from the Kremlin, consider it to be quite definite and not debatable, then why did you provoke the Civil War in Spain. Do not tell me that it was done for purely revolutionary reasons. Stalin is incapable of carrying out in practice a single Marxist theory. If there were revolutionary considerations here, then it would not be right to sacrifice in Spain so many excellent international revolutionary forces. This is the country which is furthest from the USSR, and the most elementary strategic education would not have allowed the loss of these forces... How would Stalin be able in case of conflict to supply and render military help to a Spanish Soviet republic? But this was correct. There we have an important strategic point, a crossing of opposing influences of the Capitalist States..., it might have been possible to provoke a war between them. I admit that theoretically this may have been right, but in practice— no. You already see how the war between the democratic Capitalist and fascist States did not begin. And now I shall tell you: if Stalin thought that he was capable of himself creating an excuse sufficient in order to provoke a war, in which the Capitalist States would have had to fight among themselves, then why does he not at least admit, if only theoretically, that others too can achieve the same thing, which did not seem impossible to him?...

G – If one is to agree with your assumptions then one can admit this hypothesis.

R – That means that there is yet a second point of agreement between us: the first— that there must be no war against the USSR, the second— that it would be well to provoke it between the bourgeois States.

G – Yes, I agree. Is that your personal opinion, or "Theirs"?

R – I express it as my opinion. I have no power and no contact with "Them," but I can confirm that in these two points it coincides with the view of the Kremlin.

G – That is the most important thing and for that reason it is important to establish this beforehand. By the way, I would also like to know on what you base yourself in your confidence that "They" approve this.

R. – If I had the time in order to explain their full scheme, then you would already know about the reasons for their approval. At the present moment I shall condense them to three:

G – Just which?

R – One is that which I had already mentioned. Hitler, this uneducated and elementary man, has restored thanks to his natural intuition and even against the technical opinion of Schacht, an economic system of a very dangerous kind. Being illiterate in all economic theories and being guided only by necessity he removed, as we had done it in the USSR, the private and international capital. That means that he took over for himself the privilege of manufacturing money, and not only physical moneys, but also financial ones; he took over the untouched machinery of falsification and put it to work for the benefit of the State. He exceeded us, as we, having abolished it in Russia, replaced it merely by this crude apparatus called State Capitalism; this was a very expensive triumph in view of the necessities of pre-revolutionary demagogy... Here I give you two real facts for comparison. I shall even say that Hitler had been lucky; he had almost no gold and for that reason he was not tempted to create a gold reserve. Insofar as he only possessed a full monetary guarantee of technical equipment and colossal working capacity of the Germans, his "old reserve" was technical capacity and work..., something so completely counter-revolutionary that, as you already see, he has by means of magic, as it were, radically eliminated unemployment among more than seven million technicians and workers.

G – Thanks to increased re-armament.

R – What does your re-armament give? If Hitler reached this despite all the bourgeois economists who surround him, then he was quite capable, in the absence of the danger of war, of applying his system also to peaceful production... Are you capable of imagining what would have come of this system if it had infected a number of other States and brought about the creation of a period of autarky... For example the Commonwealth. If you can, then imagine its counter-revolutionary functions... The danger is not yet inevitable, as we have had luck in that Hitler restored his system not according to some previous theory, but empirically, and he did not make any formulation of a scientific kind.* This means that insofar as he did not think in the light of a deductive process based on intelligence, he has no scientific terms or a formulated doctrine; yet there is a hidden danger as at any moment there can appear, as the consequence of deduction, a formula. This is very serious. Much more so that all the external and cruel factors in National-Socialism. We do not attack it in our propaganda as it could happen that through theoretical polemics we would ourselves provoke a formulation and systematization of this so decisive economic doctrine.** There is only one solution— war.

---

*Rakovsky is wrong, as he mentions in "Mein Kampf" Hitler had read the works of Gottfried Feder—Transl.
**The problem of a scientific formulation of this question and the propounding of a corresponding program has engaged the active attention of the publishers of this book and their associates for some years. Their conclusion has been published. In the translator's book "The Struggle for World Power," second edition 1963, p. 79 a full solution of the monetary problem is set out, and on p. 237 there is a full economic, political and social program. These conclusions can be obtained on application.

R – If the Termidor triumphed in the Soviet revolution then this happened as the result of the existence of the former Russian nationalism. Without such a nationalism Bonapartism would have been impossible. And if that happened in Russia, where nationalism was only embryonic in the person of the Tsar, then what obstacles must Marxism meet in the fully developed nationalism of Western Europe? Marx was wrong with respect to the advantages for the success of the revolution. Marxism won not in the most industrialized country, but in Russia, where the proletariat was small. Apart from other reasons our victory here is explained by the fact that in Russia there was no real nationalism, and in other countries it was in its full apogee. You see how it is reborn under this extraordinary power of fascism, and how infectious it is. You can understand that apart from that it can benefit Stalin, the need for the destruction of nationalism is alone worth a war in Europe.

G – In sum you have set out, Rakovsky, one economic and one political reason. Which is the third?

R – That is easy to guess. We have yet another reason, a religious one. Communism cannot be the victor if it will not have suppressed the still living Christianity. History speaks very clearly about this: the permanent revolution required seventeen centuries in order to achieve its first partial victory— by means of the creation of the first split in Christendom. In reality Christianity is our only real enemy, since all the political and economic phenomena in the bourgeois States are only its consequences. Christianity, controlling the individual, is capable of annulling the revolutionary projection of the neutral Soviet or atheistic State by choking it and, as we see it in Russia, things have reached the point of the creation of that spiritual nihilism which is dominant in the ruling masses, which have, nevertheless, remained Christian: this obstacle has not yet been removed during twenty years of Marxism. Let us admit in relation to Stalin that towards religion he was not Bonapartistic. We would not have done more than he and would have acted in the same way. And if Stalin had dared, like Napoleon, to cross the Rubicon of Christianity, then his nationalism and counter-revolutionary power would have been increased a thousand-fold. In addition, if this had happened then so radical a difference would have made quite impossible any collaboration in anything between us and him, even if this were to be only temporary and objective… like the one you can see becoming apparent to us.

G – And so I personally consider that you have given a definition of three fundamental points, on the basis of which a plan can be made. That is what I am in agreement about with you for the present. But I confirm to you my mental reservations, i.e. my suspicion in relation to all that which you have said concerning people, organizations and facts. Now continue to follow the general lines of your plan.

R – Yes, now this moment has arrived. But only a preliminary qualification: I shall speak on my own responsibility. I am responsible for the interpretation of those preceding points in the sense in which "They" understand them, but I admit that "They" may consider another plan to be more effective for the attainment of the three aims, and one quite unlike that which I shall now set out. Bear that in mind.

G – Very well, we shall bear it in mind. Please speak.

R – We shall simplify. Insofar as the object is missing for which the German military might had been created – to give us power in the USSR – the aim now is to bring about an advance on the fronts and to direct the Hitlerist advance not towards the East, but the West.

G – Exactly. Have you thought of the practical plan of realization?

R – I had had more than enough time for that at the Lubianka. I considered. So look: if there were difficulties in finding mutually shared points between us and all else took its normal course, then the problems comes down to again trying to establish that in which there is similarity between Hitler and Stalin.

G – Yes, but admit that all this is problematical.

R – But not insoluble, as you think. In reality problems are insoluble only when they include dialectical subjective contradictions; and even in that case we always consider possible and essential a synthesis, overcoming the "morally-impossible" of Christian metaphysicians.

G – Again you begin to theorize.

R – As the result of my intellectual discipline— this is essential for me. People of a big culture prefer to approach the concrete through a generalization, and not the other way round. With Hitler and with Stalin one can find common ground, as, being very different people, they have the same roots; if Hitler is sentimental to a pathological degree, but Stalin is normal, yet both of them are egoists: neither one of them is an idealist, and for that reason both of them are Bonapartists, i.e. classical Imperialists. And if just that is the position, then it is already not difficult to find common ground between them. Why not, if it proved possible between one Tsarina and one Prussian King...

G – Rakovsky, you are incorrigible...

R – You do not guess? If Poland was the point of union between Catherine and Frederick— the Tsarina of Russia and the King of Germany at that time, then why cannot Poland serve as a reason for the finding of common ground between Hitler and Stalin? In Poland the persons of Hitler and Stalin can coincide. and also the historical Tsarist Bolshevik and Nazi lines. Our line, "Their" line— also, as Poland is a Christian State and, what makes the matter even more complex, a Catholic one.

G – And what follows from the fact of such a treble coincidence?

R – If there is common ground then there is a possibility of agreement.

G – Between Hitler and Stalin?... Absurd! Impossible.

R – In politics there are neither absurdities, nor the impossible.

G – Let us imagine, as an hypothesis: Hitler and Stalin advance on Poland.

R – Permit me to interrupt you; an attack can be called forth only by the following alternative: war or peace. You must admit it.

G – Well, and so what?

R – Do you consider that England and France, with their worse armies and aviation, in comparison with Hitler's, can attack the united Hitler and Stalin?

G – Yes, that seems to me to be very difficult... unless America...

R – Let us leave the United States aside for the moment. Will you agree with me that as the result of the attack of Hitler and Stalin on Poland there can be no European war?

G – You argue logically; it would seem impossible.

R – In that case an attack or war would be useless. It would not call forth the mutual destruction of the bourgeois States: the Hitlerist threat to the USSR would continue in being after the division of Poland since theoretically both Germany and the USSR would have been strengthened to the same extent. In practice Hitler to a greater extent since the USSR does not need more land and raw materials for its strengthening, but Hitler does need them.

G – This is a correct view…, but I can see no other solution.

R – No, there is a solution.

G – Which?

R – That the democracies should attack and not attack the aggressor.

G – What are you saying, what hallucination! Simultaneously to attack and not to attack… That is something absolutely impossible.

R – You think so? Calm down… Are there not two aggressors? Did we not agree that there will be no advance just because there are two? Well… What prevents the attack on one of them?

G – What do you want to say by that?

R – Simply that the democracies will declare war only on one aggressor, and that will be Hitler.

G – Yes, but that is an unfounded hypothesis.

R – An hypothesis, but having a foundation. Consider: each State which will have to fight with a coalition of enemy States has as its main strategic objective to destroy them separately one after another. This rule is so well known that proofs are superfluous. So, agree with me that there are no obstacles to the creation of such conditions. I think that the question that Stalin will not consider himself aggrieved in case of an attack on Hitler is already settled. Is that not so? In addition geography imposes this attitude, and for that reason strategy also. However stupid France and England may be in preparing to fight simultaneously against two countries, one of which wants to preserve its neutrality, while the other, even being alone, represents for them a serious opponent, from where and from which side could they carry out an attack on the USSR? They have not got a common border; unless they were to advance over the Himalayas… Yes, there remains the air front, but with what forces and from where could they invade Russia? In comparison with Hitler they are weaker in the air. All the arguments I have mentioned are no secret and are well known. As you see, all is simplified to a considerable extent.

G – Yes, your arguments seem to be logical in the case if the conflict will be limited to four countries; but there are not four, but more, and neutrality is not a simple matter in a war on the given scale.

R – Undoubtedly, but the possible participation of many countries does not change the power relationships. Weigh this in your mind and you will see how the balance will continue, even if others or even all European States come in. In addition, and this is very important, not one of those States, which will enter the war at the side of England and France will be able to deprive them of leadership; as a result the reasons which will prevent their attack on the USSR will retain their significance.

G – You forget about the United States.

R – In a moment you will see that I have not forgotten. I shall limit myself to the investigation of their function in the preliminary program, which occupies us at present, and I shall say that America will not be able to force France and England to attack Hitler and Stalin simultaneously. In order to attain that the United States would have to enter the war from the very first day. But that is impossible. In the first place because America did not enter a war formerly and never will do so if it is not attacked. Its rulers can arrange that they will be attacked, if that will suit them. Of that I can assure you. In those cases when provocation was not successful and the enemy did not react to it, aggression was invented. In their first international war, the war against Spain, of the defeat of which they were sure, they invented an aggression, or, more correctly, "They" invented it. In 1914 provocation was successful. True, one can dispute technically if there was one, but the rule without exceptions is that he who makes a sudden attack without warning, does it with the help of a provocation. Now it is like this: this splendid American technique which I welcome at any moment, is subject to one condition: that aggression should take place at a suitable moment, i.e. the moment required by the United States who are being attacked; that means then, when they will have the arms. Does this condition exist now? It is clear that it does not. In America there are at present a little less than one hundred thousand men under arms and a middling aviation: it has only an imposing fleet. But you can understand that, having it, it cannot persuade its allies to decide on an attack on the USSR, since England and France have preponderance only at sea. I have also proved to you that from that side there can be no change in the comparative strengths of the forces.

G – Having agreed with this, I ask you again to explain once more the technical realization.

R – As you have seen, given the coincidence of the interests of Stalin and Hitler with regard to an attack on Poland, all comes down to the formalization of this full similarity of aims and to make a pact about a double attack.

G – And you think this is easy?

R – Frankly, no. Here we need a diplomacy which is more experienced than that of Stalin. There ought to have been available the one which Stalin had decapitated, or the one which now decays in the Lubianka. In former times Litvinov would have been capable, with some difficulties, although his race would have been a great obstacle for negotiations with Hitler; but now this is a finished man and he is destroyed by a terrible panic; he is experiencing an animal fear of Molotov, even more than of Stalin. His whole talent is directed towards making sure that they should not think that he is a Trotskyist. If he were to hear of the necessity of arranging closer relations with Hitler, then that would be enough for him to manufacture for himself the proof of his Trotskyism. I do not see a man who is capable of this job; in any event he would have to be a pure-blooded Russian. I could offer my services for guidance. At the present moment I would suggest to the one who begins the talks, that they should be strictly confidential, but with great open sincerity. Given a whole wall of various prejudices only truthfulness can deceive Hitler.

G – I again do not understand your paradoxical expressions.

R – Forgive me, but this only appears to be so; I am forced by the synthesis to do so. I wanted to say that with Hitler one must play a clean game concerning the concrete and most immediate questions. It is necessary to show him that the game is not played in order to provoke him into war on two fronts. For example, it is possible to promise him and to prove at the most suitable moment that our mobilization will be limited to a small number of forces, required for the invasion of Poland, and that these forces will not be great. According to our real plan we shall have to place our main forces to meet the possible Anglo French attack. Stalin will have to be generous with the preliminary supplies which Hitler will demand, chiefly oil. That is what has come to my mind for the moment. Thousands of further questions will arise, of a similar character, which will have to be solved so that Hitler, seeing in practice that we only want to occupy our part of Poland, would be quite certain of that. And insofar as in practice it should be just like that, he will be deceived by the truth.

G – But in what, in this case, is there a deception?

R – I shall give you a few minutes of time so that you yourself can discover just in what there is a deception of Hitler. But first I want to stress, and you should take note, that the plan which I have indicated here, is logical and normal and I think that one can achieve that the Capitalistic States will destroy each other, if one brings about a clash of their two wings: the fascist and the bourgeois. I repeat that the plan is logical and normal. As you have already been able to see, there is no intervention here of mysterious or unusual factors. In short in order that one should be able to realize the plan, "Their" intervention is not required. Now I should like to guess your thoughts: are you not now thinking that it would be stupid to waste time on proving the unprovable existence and power held by "Them." Is that not so?

G – You are right.

R – Be frank with me. Do you really not observe their intervention? I informed you, wanting to help you that their intervention exists and is decisive, and for that reason the logic and naturalness, of the plan are only appearances… Is it really true that you do not see "Them"?

G – Speaking sincerely, no.

R – The logic and naturalness of my plan is only an appearance. It would be natural and logical that Hitler and Stalin would inflict defeat on each other. For the democracies that would be a simple and easy thing, if they would have to put forward such an aim, for them it would be enough that Hitler should be permitted, make note "permitted" to attack Stalin. Do not tell me that Germany could be defeated. If the Russian distances and the dreadful fear of Stalin and his henchmen of the Hitlerite axe and the revenge of their victims will not be enough in order to attain the military exhaustion of Germany, then there will be no obstacles to the democracies, seeing that Stalin is losing strength, beginning to help him wisely and methodically, continuing to give that help until the complete exhaustion of both armies. In reality that would be easy, natural and logical, if those motives and aims which are put forward by the democracies and which most of their followers believe to be the true ones, and not what they are in reality— pretexts. There is only one aim, one single aim: the triumph of Communism; it is not Moscow which will impose its will on the democracies, but New York, not the "Comintern," but the "Capintern" on Wall Street. Who other that he could have been able to impose on Europe such an obvious and absolute contradiction? What force can lead it towards complete suicide? Only one force is able to do this: money. Money is power and the sole power.

G – I shall be frank with you, Rakovsky. I admit in you an exceptional gift of talent. You possess brilliant dialectic, persuasive and subtle: when this is not enough for you, then your imagination has command of means in order to extend your colorful canvas, while you invent brilliant and clear perspectives; but all this, although it provokes my enthusiasm, is not enough for me. I shall go over to putting questions to you, assuming that I believe all that you have said.

R – And I shall give you replies, but with one single condition, that you should not add anything to what I shall say, nor deduct.

G – I promise. You assert that "They" hinder or will hinder a German-Soviet war, which is logical from the point of view of the Capitalists. Have I explained it correctly?

R – Yes, precisely so.

G – But the reality of the present moment is such that Germany has been permitted to re-arm and expand. This is a fact. I already know that in accordance with your explanation this was called forth by the Trotskyist plan, which fell through thanks to the "cleanings-out" now taking place; thus the aim has been lost. In the face of a new situation you only advise that Hitler and Stalin should sign a pact and divide Poland. I ask you: how can we obtain a guarantee that, having the pact, or not having it, carrying out, or not carrying out the partition, Hitler will not attack the USSR?

R – This cannot be guaranteed.

G – Then why go on talking?

R – Do not hurry. The magnificent threat to the USSR is real and exists. This is not an hypothesis and not a verbal threat. It is a fact and a fact which obliges. "They" already have superiority over Stalin, a superiority which cannot be denied. Stalin is offered only one alternative, the right to choose, but not full freedom. The attack of Hitler will come in any case of its own accord; "They" need not do anything to make it happen but only leave him the chance of acting. This is the basic and determining reality, which has been forgotten by you owing to your excessively Kremlin-like way of thinking... Egocentrism, Sir, egocentrism.

G – The right to choose?

R – I shall define it exactly once more, but shortly: either there will be an attack on Stalin, or there will come the realization of the plan I have indicated, according to which the European Capitalistic States will destroy each other. I drew attention to this alternative, but as you see it was only a theoretical one. If Stalin wants to survive then he will be forced to realize the plan which has been proposed by me and ratified by "Them."

G – But if he refuses?

R – That will be impossible for him. The expansion and re-armament of Germany will continue. When Stalin will be faced by this gigantic threat…, then what will he do? This will be dictated to him by his own instinct of self-preservation.

G – It seems that events must develop only according to the orders indicated by "Them."

R – And it is so. Of course, in the USSR today things still stand like this, but sooner or later it will happen like that all the same. It is not difficult to foretell and to suggest for carrying out something, if it is profitable for the person who must realize the matter, in the given case Stalin, who is hardly thinking of suicide. It is much more difficult to give a prognosis and to force to act as needed someone for whom that is not profitable, but who must act nevertheless, in the given case the democracies. I have kept the explanation for this moment to give a concrete picture of the true position. Reject the wrong thought that you are the arbiters in the given situation, since "They" are the arbiters.

G – "They" both in the first and the second case… Therefore we must deal with shadows?

R – But are facts shadows? The international situation will be extraordinary, but not shadowy; it is real and very real. This is not a miracle; here is predetermined the future policy… Do you think this is the work of shadows?

G – But let us see; let us assume that your plan is accepted… But we must have something tangible, personal, in order to be able to carry out negotiations.

R – For example?

G – Some person with powers of attorney and representation.

R – But for what? Just for the pleasure of becoming acquainted with him? For the pleasure of a talk? Bear in mind that the assumed person, in case of his appearance, will not present you with credentials with seals and crests and will not wear a diplomatic uniform, at least a man from "Them"; if he were to say something or promise, then it will have no Juridical force or meaning as a pact… Understand that "They" are not a State; "They" are that which the International was before 1917, that which it still is nothing and at the same time everything. Imagine to yourself if it is possible that the USSR would have negotiations with freemasonry, with an espionage organization, with the Macedonian Komitadgi or the Croatian Ustashi. Would not some Juridical agreement be written?… Such pacts as the pact of Lenin with the German General Staff, as the pact of Trotsky with "Them"— are realized without written documents and without signatures. The only guarantee of their execution is rooted in the circumstance that the carrying out of that which has been agreed is profitable for the parties to the pact, this guarantee is the sole reality in the pact, however great may be its importance.

G – From what would you begin in the present case?

R – Simple; I should begin already from tomorrow to sound out Berlin…

G – In order to agree about the attack on Poland?

R – I would not begin with that… I would display my willingness to yield and would hint about certain disappointments among the democracies, I would soft-pedal in Spain… This would be an act of encouragement; then I would drop a hint about Poland. As you see— nothing compromising, but enough so that a part of the OKW (German High Command —Transl.), the Bismarckists, as they are called, would have some arguments to put before Hitler.

G – And nothing more?

R – For the beginning, nothing more; this is already a big diplomatic task.

G – Speaking frankly, having in mind the aims which have been dominant in the Kremlin until now, I do not think that anyone would at present dare to advise such a radical change in international policy. I propose to you, Rakovsky, to transform yourself in imagination into that person at the Kremlin which will have to take the decision… On the basis only of your disclosures, arguments, your hypotheses and persuasion, as I see it, it would be impossible to convince anyone. I personally, after having listened to you and at the same time, I shall not deny it, having experienced a strong influence from your explanations, of your personality, have not for a single moment experienced the temptation to consider the German-Soviet pact to be something realizable.

R – International events will force with irresistible strength…

G – But that would be a loss of valuable time. Consider something concrete, something which I could put forward as a proof of your veracity and credibility… In the contrary case I should not dare to transmit your information about our conversation; I should edit it with all accuracy, but it would reach the Kremlin archives and stay there.

R – Would it not be enough to bring about that it is taken into consideration if someone, even in a most official manner, were to have a talk with some very important person?

G – It seems to me that this would be something real.

R – But with whom?

G – This is only my personal opinion, Rakovsky. You had mentioned concrete persons, big financiers; if I remember correctly, you had spoken about a certain Schiff, for example; then you mentioned another who had been the go-between with Hitler for the purpose of financing him. There are also politicians or persons with a big position, who belong to "Them" or, if you like, serve "Them." Someone like that could be of use to us in order to start something practical… Do you know someone?

R – I do not think it is necessary… Think: about what will you be negotiating? Probably about the plan which I have set out, is that not so? For what? At the present moment "They" need not do anything in this context; "Their" mission is "not to do." And for that reason you would not be able to agree about any positive action and could not demand it… Remember, consider well.

G – Even if that is so, yet in view of our personal opinion there must be a reality, even if a useless one..., a man, a personality which would confirm the credibility of the power, which you ascribe to "Them."

R – I shall satisfy you, although I am sure of the uselessness of this. I have already told you that I do not know who is a part of "Them," but have assurances from a person who must have known them.

G – From whom?

R – From Trotsky. From Trotsky I know only that one of "Them" was Walter Rathenau, who was well known from Rapallo. You see the last of "Them" who occupied a political and social position, since it was he who broke the economic blockade of the USSR. Despite the fact that he was one of the biggest millionaires; of course, such also was Lionel Rothschild. I can with confidence mention only these names. Naturally I can name still more people, the work and personality of whom I determine as being fully "Theirs," but I cannot confirm what these people command or whom they obey.

G – Mention some of them.

R – As an institutions— the Bank of Kuhn, Loeb & Co., of Wall Street; to this bank belong the families of Schiff, Warburg, Loeb and Kuhn; I say families in order to point out several names, since they are all connected among themselves by marriages; then Baruch, Frankfurter, Altschul, Cohen, Benjamin, Strauss, Steinhardt, Blom, Rosenman, Lippmann, Lehman, Dreifus, Lamont, Rothschild, Lord, Mandel Morgenthau, Ezekiel, Lasky. I think that that will be enough names; if I were to strain my memory, then perhaps I would remember some more but I repeat, that I do not know who among them can be one of "Them" and I cannot even assert, that any one of them is definitely of their number; I want to avoid any responsibility. But I certainly think that any one of the persons I have enumerated, even of those not belonging to "Them," could always lead to "Them" with any proposition of an important type. Of course, independently of whether this or that person does or does not belong to "Them," one cannot expect a direct reply. The answer will be given by facts. That is the unchangeable tactic which they prefer and with which they force one to reckon. For example, if you would risk beginning diplomatic initiatives, then you would not need to make use of the method of a personal approach to "Them"; one must limit oneself to the expression of thoughts, the exposition of some rational hypothesis, which depends on unknown definite factors. Then it only remains to wait.

G – You understand that I have not got a card-index at my disposal at the moment, in order to establish all the men you have mentioned: I assume that they are probably somewhere far away. Where?

R – Most of them in the United States.

G – Please understand that if we were to decide to act, then we would have to devote much time to it. But the matter is urgent, and urgent not for us, but for you, Rakovsky.

R – For me?

G – Yes, for you. Remember that your trial will take place very soon. I do not know, but I think it will not be risky to assume that if all that had been discussed here were to interest the Kremlin, then it must interest them before you appear before the tribunal: that would be for you a decisive matter. I think it is in your personal interests that you should propose something quicker to us. The most important thing is to get proofs that you spoke the truth, and to do this not during a period of several weeks, but during several days. I think that if you were to succeed in this, then I could nearly give you fairly solid assurances concerning the possibility of saving your life... In the contrary case I answer for nothing.

R – In the end I shall take the risk. Do you know if Davis is at present in Moscow? Yes, the Ambassador of the United States.

G – I think he is; he should have returned.

R – Only an exceptional situation gives me the right, as I see it, against the rules, to make use of an official intermediary.

G – Therefore we can think that the American Government is behind all this...

R – Behind— no under all this...

G – Roosevelt?

R – What do I know? I can only come to conclusions. You are all the time obsessed with the mania of political espionage. I could manufacture, in order to please you, a whole history; I have more than sufficient imagination, dates and true facts in order to give it veracity in appearance, which would be close to looking obvious. But are not the generally known facts more obvious? And you can supplement them with your own imagination, if you wish. Look yourself. Remember the morning of the 24th October 1929. The time will come when this day will be for the history of the revolution more important than October, 1917. On the day of the 24th October there took place the crash of the New York Stock Exchange, the beginning of the so-called "depression," a real revolution. The four years of the Government of Hoover— are years of revolutionary progress: 12 and 15 million on strike. In February, 1933 there takes place the last stroke of the crisis with the closing of the banks. It is difficult to do more than capital did in order to break the "classical American," who was still on his industrial bases and in the economic respect enslaved by Wall Street. It is well known that any impoverishment in economics, be it in relation to societies or animals, gives a flourishing of parasitism, and capital is a large parasite. But this American revolution pursued not only the one aim of increasing the power of money for those who had the right to use it, it pretended to even more. Although the power of money is political power, but before that it had only been used indirectly, but now the power of money was to be transformed into direct power. The man through whom they made use of such power was Franklin Roosevelt. Have you understood? Take note of the following: In that year 1929, the first year of the American revolution in February Trotsky leaves Russia; the crash takes place in October... The financing of Hitler is agreed in July, 1929. You think that all this was by chance? The four years of the rule of Hoover were used for the preparation of the seizure of power in the United States and the USSR; there by means of a financial revolution and here with the help of war and the defeat which was to follow. Could some good novel with great imagination be more obvious to you? You can understand that the execution of the plan on such a scale requires a special man, who can direct the executive power in the United States, who has been predetermined to be the organizing and deciding force. That man was Franklin and Eleanor Roosevelt. And permit me to say that this two-sexed being is not simply irony. He had to avoid any possible Delilah.

G – Is Roosevelt one of "Them"?

R – I do not know if he is one of "Them," or is only subject to "Them." What more do you want? I think that he was conscious of his mission, but cannot assert whether he obeyed under duress of blackmail or he was one of those who rule; it is true that he carried out his mission, realized all the actions which had been assigned to him accurately. Do not ask me more, as I do not know any more.

G – In case it should be decided to approach Davis, in which form would you do it?

R – First of all you must select a person of such a type as "the baron"; he could be useful... Is he still alive?

G – I do not know.

R – All right, the choice of persons is left to you. Your delegate must present himself as being confidential or not modest, but best of all as a secret oppositionist. The conversation must be cleverly conducted concerning that contradictory position into which the USSR has been put by the so-called European democracies, by their union against National-Socialism. This is the conclusion of an alliance with the British and French Imperialism, the contemporary real Imperialism, for the destruction of the potential Imperialism. The aim of the verbal expressions must be to conjoin the false Soviet position with an equally false one of American democracy... It also sees itself forced to support Colonial Imperialism for the defense of democracy within England and France. As you see, the question can be put onto a very strong logical foundation. After that it is already very easy to formulate an hypothesis about actions. The first: that neither the USSR, nor the United States are interested in European Imperialism and thus the dispute is brought down to the question of personal hegemony; that ideologically and economically Russia and America want the destruction of European Colonial Imperialism, be it direct or oblique. The United States want it even more. If Europe were to lose all its power in a new war, then England, not having its own forces, with the disappearance of Europe as a force, as power, would from the first day lean, with all its weight and with the whole of its Empire, speaking the English language, on the United States, which would be inevitable both in the political and economic sense... Analyze what you have heard in the light of the Left conspiracy, as one might say, without shocking any American bourgeois. Having got to this point, one could have an interval for a few days. Then, having noted the reaction, it will be necessary to move further. Now Hitler comes forward. Here one can point to any aggression: he is fully an aggressor and of this there can be no doubt. And then one can go over to asking a question: What common action should be undertaken by the United States and the Soviet Union in view of the war between the Imperialists, who want it? The answer could be— neutrality. One must argue again: yes, neutrality, but it does not depend on the wish of one side, but also of the aggressor. There can be a guarantee of neutrality only when the aggressor cannot attack or it does not suit him. For this purpose the infallible answer is the attack of the aggressor on another Imperialist State. From this it is very easy to go over to the expression of the necessity and morality, with a view to guaranteeing safety, for provoking a clash between the Imperialists, if that clash were not to take place of its own accord. And if that were to be accepted in theory, and it will be accepted, then one can regulate the question of actions in practice, which would be only a matter of technique. Here is a scheme: (1) A pact with Hitler for the division between us of Czechoslovakia and Poland (better the latter). (2) Hitler will accept. If he is capable of backing a bluff for the conquest, i.e. the seizure of something in alliance with the USSR, then for him there will be full guarantee in that the democracies will yield. He will be unable to believe their verbal threats as he knows that those who try to intimidate by war threats are at the same time partisans of disarmament and that their disarmament is real. (3) The democracies will attack Hitler and not Stalin; they will tell the people that although both are guilty of aggression and partition, but strategic and logical reasons force them to defeat them one by one: first Hitler and then Stalin.

G – But will they not deceive us with truth?

R – But how? Does not Stalin dispose of freedom of action in order to help Hitler in sufficient measure? Do we not put in his hands the possibility of continuing the war between the Capitalists until the last man and the last pound? With what can they attack him? The exhausted States of the West will already have enough on their hands with internal Communist revolution, which in the other case may triumph.

G – But if Hitler achieves a quick victory and if he, like Napoleon, mobilizes the whole of Europe against the USSR?

R – This is quite improbable! You forget about the existence of the United States. You reject the power factor, a greater one. Is it not natural that America, imitating Stalin, would on its part help the democratic States? If one were to co-ordinate "against the hands of the clock" the help to both groups of fighters, then thus there will be assured without failure a permanent extension of the war.

G – And Japan?

R – Is not China enough for them? Let Stalin guarantee them his non-intervention. The Japanese are very fond of suicide, but after all not to such an extent as to be capable of simultaneously attacking China and the USSR. Any more objections?

G – No, if it were to depend on me, then I would try... But do you believe that the delegate...?

R – Yes, I believe. I was not given the chance of speaking with him, but note one detail: the appointment of Davis became known in November, 1936; we must assume that Roosevelt thought of sending him much sooner and with that in mind began preliminary steps; we all know that the consideration of the matter and the official explanations of the appointment take more than two months. Apparently his appointment was agreed in August... And what happened in August? In August Zinoviev and Kamenev were shot. I am willing to swear that his appointment was made for the purpose of a new involvement of "Them' in the politics of Stalin. Yes, I certainly think so. With what an inner excitement must he have traveled, seeing how one after another there fall the chiefs of the opposition in the "purges" which follow one on another. Do you know if he was present at trial of Radeck?

G – Yes.

R – You will see him. Have a talk with him. He expects it already for many months.

G – This night we must finish; but before we part I want to know something more.

Let us assume that all this is true and all will be carried out with full success. "They" will put forward definite conditions. Guess what they might be?

R – This is not difficult to assume. The first condition will be the ending of the executions of the Communists, that means the Trotskyists, as you call them. Then, of course, they will demand the establishment of several zones of influence, as I had mentioned. The boundaries which will have to divide the formal Communism from the real one. That is the most important condition. There will be mutual concessions for mutual help for a time, while the plan lasts, being carried out. You will see for example the paradoxical phenomenon that a whole crowd of people, enemies of Stalin, will help him, no they will not necessarily be proletarians, nor will they be professional spies. There will appear influential persons at all levels of society, even very high ones, who will help the Stalinist formal Communism when it becomes if not real, then at least objective Communism. Have you understood me?

G – A little; you wrap up such things in such impenetrable casuistry.

R – If it is necessary to end, then I can only express myself in this way. Let us see if I shall not be able yet to help to understand. It is known that Marxism was called Hegelian. So this question was vulgarized. Hegelian idealism is a widespread adjustment to an uninformed understanding in the West of the natural mysticism of Baruch Spinoza. "They" are Spinozists: perhaps the matter is the other way round, i.e. that Spinozism is "Them," insofar as he is only a version adequate to the epoch of "Their" own philosophy, which is a much earlier one, standing on a much higher level. After all, a Hegelian and for that reason also the follower of Spinoza, was devoted to his faith, but only temporarily, tactically. The matter does not stand as is claimed by Marxism, that as the result of the elimination of contradictions there arises the synthesis. It is as the result of the opposing mutual fusion, from the thesis and anti-thesis that there arises, as a synthesis, the reality, truth. as a final harmony between the subjective and objective. Do you not see that already? In Moscow there is Communism: in New York Capitalism. It is all the same as a thesis and anti-thesis. Analyze both. Moscow is subjective Communism, but Capitalism – objective – State Capitalism. New York: Capitalism subjective, but Communism objective. A personal synthesis, truth: the Financial International, the Capitalist-Communist one. "They."

* * *

The meeting had lasted about six hours. I once more gave some drug to Rakovsky. The drug it was obvious, worked well, although I was only able to observe this by certain symptoms of animation. But I think that Rakovsky would have spoken just the same in a normal condition. Undoubtedly the theme of the conversation concerned his specialty and he had the passionate will to espouse that, about which he spoke. Since, if all this is true then an energetic attempt had been made to enforce the triumph of his idea and plan. If this was untrue, then there was an extraordinary fantasy and this was a wonderful maneuver for saving his already lost life.

My opinion of all that had been heard cannot be of any importance. I have not got a sufficient erudition in order to understand its universality and horizons. When Rakovsky touched on the most important part of the theme I had the same feeling as at that moment when I saw myself for the first time on the X-ray screen. My surprised eyes saw something diffuse and dark, but real. Something like an apparition; I had to coordinate his figure and movements, correlations and actions to the degree to which it was possible to guess with the help of logical intuition.

I think that I had observed during several hours the "radiograph of revolution" on a world-wide scale. It is possible that in part it failed, was deformed, thanks to circumstances or personalities which reflected it, it is not for nothing that the lie and dissimulation are permitted in the revolutionary struggle and are accepted as moral. And Rakovsky, a passionate dialectician of great culture and a first-class orator, is first of all and above all a revolutionary fanatic.

I re-read the conversation many times, but each time I felt how there rose in me the feeling of my incompetence in this respect. That which until then had seemed to me, and to the whole world, to be the truth and obvious reality, like blocks of granite, where the social order stands as on a rock, immovable and permanent, all that became transformed into a thick fog. There appear colossal, immeasurable, invisible forces with a categorical imperative, disobedient, sly and titanic at the same time, something like magnetism, electricity or the attraction of the earth. In the presence of this phenomenal disclosure I felt like the man from the Stone Age, whose head was still full of primitive superstitions concerning the phenomena of nature, and who had been suddenly transposed one night into the Paris of today. I am amazed even more than he would have been.

Many times I disagreed. At first I convinced myself that everything which Rakovsky was telling was the product of his extraordinary imagination. But even having convinced myself that I was a toy in the hands of the biggest of all the writers of novels, I tried in vain to find enough strength, logical reasons and even people with a sufficient personality, who would have been able to explain this gigantic progress of the revolution.

I must confess that if only those forces participated here, as also reasons and people, which are mentioned officially in written histories, then I must declare that the revolution is a miracle of our age. No, when I was listening to Rakovsky, I could not admit that a small group of Jews, who emigrated from London, had achieved that this "apparition of revolution," which had been called forth by Marx in the first lines of the Manifesto, had become today a gigantic reality and a universal threat.

Whether what Rakovsky told is true or not, whether the secret and real strength of Communism is International Capital, it is the obvious truth for me that Marx, Lenin, Trotsky and Stalin are an insufficient explanation for that which is happening.

Whether these people are real or fantastic, whom Rakovsky calls "Them" with an almost religious tremor in his voice, is the question. But if "They" do not exist then I shall have to say of them what Voltaire said of God: "He will have to be invented," since only in that case can we explain the existence, extent and force of this world-wide revolution.

After all, I have no hope of seeing it. My position does not allow me to view with great optimism the possibility that I shall survive until the near future. But this suicide of the bourgeois European States, of which Rakovsky spoke, and which he proves as being inevitable, would be for me, who has been initiated into the secret, the magisterial and definite proof.

* * *

When Rakovsky had been led away to his place of imprisonment Gabriel remained some time immersed in himself.

I looked at him, not seeing him; and in fact my own ideas and conceptions had lost the ground under their feet and were somehow suspended.

"How do you look on all this" asked Gabriel.

"I do not know, I do not know" I replied, and I spoke the truth; but I added "I think that this is an amazing man and if we are dealing with a falsification, then it is extraordinary; in any event it is a piece of genius."

"As a result, if we shall have the time, we must have an exchange of views... I am always interested in your opinion of the profane, a doctor. But now we must agree about our program. I need you as a professional, but as a modest man. That which you have heard, as the result of your peculiar function, can be wind and smoke which is carried by the wind, but it can also be something, the importance of which cannot be exceeded by anything else. Here a moderate terminology is inappropriate. Given this last possibility, a strong feeling of precaution forces me to limit the number of people who know about it. For the moment only you and I know. The man who manipulated the recording machine does not know any French. The fact that we did not speak in Russian was not my caprice. In short: I shall be grateful to you if you will be the translator. Sleep for some hours. I shall now give the necessary instructions so that the technician would agree the time with you, and as soon as possible you must translate and write down the conversation, which he will reproduce for you to hear. It will be a hard job; you cannot use a typewriter and the recorder will have to move very slowly. When you will have done the French version I shall read it. A few remarks and epigraphs will be necessary, and I shall add them. You can use a typewriter?"

"Very badly, very slowly, only with two fingers."

"Well arrange it somehow. Please make few mistakes."

Gabriel called the man. We arranged to begin work at eleven o'clock and it was already almost seven. We went to sleep a little.

I was called punctually. We sat down in my small study.

Gabriel had asked me to make two copies of the translation. I made three, in order to hide one for myself. I took the risk as he went to Moscow. I am not sorry that I had had the courage for this.

EPILOGUE

As is well known, Stalin followed the advice of Rakovsky. There was a pact with Hitler. Also the Second World War served solely the interests of the revolution.

The secret of these changes of policy can be understood from a further conversation between Gabriel and Doctor Landowsky, which is given in a later chapter of "The Red Symphony." Here are some extracts from it:

GABRIEL – Do you remember the conversation with Rakovsky... Do you know that he was not condemned to death? Well knowing all this you need not be surprised that Comrade Stalin had thought it to be wise to try that apparently so unlikely plan... Here nothing is risked and, on the contrary, one can gain a great deal... If you will strain your memory you will be able to understand several things.

DOCTOR – I remember everything rather well. Do not forget that I heard the conversation twice, then both times I wrote it, and in addition I translated it... May I find out if you know the people whom Rakovsky called "Them"?

G – In order to show you my confidence I shall tell you— no! We do not know for sure who "They" are, but at the last moment there was confirmed a great deal of what Rakovsky had told; for example it is true that Hitler was financed by the Wall Street bankers. Much else is also true. All these months, during which I have not seen you, I devoted to an investigation, connected with Rakovsky's information. It is true that I was not able to establish just which people are such remarkable personages, but it is a fact, that there is a kind of entourage which consists of financiers, politicians, scientists and even ecclesiastical persons of high rank, wealth and power, who occupy high places; if one is to judge their position (mostly as intermediaries) by the results, then it seems strange and inexplicable, at least in the light of ordinary conceptions... since in fact they have a great similarity with the ideas of Communism, of course with very special Communist ideas. But let us leave all these questions aside, concerning complexion, line and profile; objectively, as Rakovsky would have said, they, imitating Stalin blindly in actions and errors, are building Communism. They followed the advice of Rakovsky almost to the letter. There was nothing concrete, but there was no refusal and no tearing of mantles. On the contrary, they displayed great attention to everything. The Ambassador Davis carefully hinted at the past trials and even went so far as to hint that much would be gained in the public opinion in America, in case of an amnesty for Rakovsky in the near future. He was well watched during the trials in March, which is natural. He was himself present at all of them; we did not allow him to bring any technicians so as to prevent any "telegraphing" with the accused. He is not a professional diplomat and does not know the specific techniques. He was obliged to look on, trying with his eyes to say much, as I thought; we think that he raised the spirits of Rosenholz and of Rakovsky. The latter confirmed the interest which had been displayed at the trial by Davis and confessed that he made him a secret sign of Masonic greeting.

There is yet another strange matter, which cannot be falsified. On the 2nd March at dawn there was received a radio message from some very powerful station: "Amnesty or the Nazi danger will increase"... the radiogram was enciphered in the cypher of our own embassy in London. You can understand that that was something very important!

Dr – But the threat was not real?

G – How not? On the 12th March there ended the debates of the Supreme Tribunal and at 9 in the evening the tribunal began its considerations. And on that same day of the 12th March, at 5:30 o'clock a.m. Hitler ordered his armored divisions to enter Austria. Of course this was a military promenade! Were there sufficient reasons for thinking about that! Or we had to be so stupid as to consider the greetings of Davis, the radio program, the cypher, the coincidence of the invasion with the verdict, and also the silence of Europe as being only accidental chances? No, in fact we did not see "Them," but we heard their voice and understood their language.

* * *

Translator's note: It would be quite superfluous to write a long commentary on this remarkable material. It should suffice to say the obvious— this is one of the most important political documents of the century.

Many of us have known the facts here brought out for decades, but for the first time we get a brilliant, detailed statement from an insider. Obviously Rakovsky was one of "Them."

Both the internal evidence of this document, as well as the circumstance that all subsequent events went exactly according to the formulae indicated proves the truth of the story.

This book should be essential reading for all who wish to know what is happening and why, throughout the world, and also what alone can be done to stop the conquests of the revolution: the power of monetary emission must be returned to the States everywhere. If that is not done in time, Communism will win.

George Knupffer

Printed at Repro India Ltd.